HOW TO SAVE OUR DEMOCRACY

TIMOTHY J. HEAPHY

STEERFORTH PRESS
LEBANON, NEW HAMPSHIRE

Endnotes for *We Are the Answer*, featuring sourcing citations, are available online at wearetheanswer.steerforth.com.

Steerforth Press
An imprint of Pushkin Press
254 Plainfield Rd Unit 11, #1063
West Lebanon, NH 03784

The contents of this book have been adapted from *Harbingers: What January 6 and Charlottesville Reveal about Rising Threats to American Democracy*, by Timothy J. Heaphy, which was published in hardcover in 2025

Cataloging-in-Publication Data is available from the Library of Congress

www.pushkinpress.com

ISBN 978-1-58642-456-5 (paperback)

Printed in the United States of America

The authorized representative in the EEA is eucomply OÜ, Pärnu mnt. 139b-14, 11317, Tallinn, Estonia, hello@eucompliancepartner.com, +33757690241

1 3 5 7 9 10 8 6 4 2

"Timothy Heaphy's ideas about our country's future should be listened to by all." — **John Grisham**

"Heaphy's deeply informed work is essential reading for all who hope to learn from the past so we don't repeat it." — **James Comey, former FBI director and author of *A Higher Loyalty***

"A soulful and significant contribution to defeating the authoritarian threat in America." — **Congressman Jamie Raskin, author of *Unthinkable***

"I urge you to read this book, then do your part." — **Adam Kinzinger, author of *Renegade***

"Heaphy's insights can help us reclaim a government that works for all Americans and restore faith in our democratic institutions." — **Barbara McQuade, author of *Attack from Within***

"Amid our nation's bitter political divisions, Heaphy offers a hopeful message." — **Carol Leonnig, author of *Zero Fail***

"In this highly readable book, Heaphy points constructive paths forward toward a healthier and more hopeful future." — **David Von Drehle, author of *The Book of Charlie***

"A must-read for anyone who wants to understand the toxic ideologies and violent threats lurking just beneath the surface of our fractured politics." — **Nicolle Wallace, host of MSNBC's *Deadline: White House***

"An essential read to build a path forward free from political violence." — **Preet Bharara, author of *Doing Justice***

"Important suggestions about how we can all do better, both inside and outside government." — **Glenn Kirschner**

"Heaphy provides solutions to make sure our democracy stays intact. A must-read." — **Senator Tim Kaine**

"Heaphy's prescriptions, born of experience, should be required reading for anyone interested in preserving — and improving — participatory democracy on these shores." — **Robert Edwards, author of *Resisting the Right***

"If citizens are wise enough to follow Heaphy's prescription for change, Americans will have a chance to cure what ails us before more damage is done." — **Larry J. Sabato, director, UVA Center for Politics**

CONTENTS

INTRODUCTION

Reluctant Expert

Over the course of my career, I've learned that lawyers often become accidental specialists. The matters on which they work, the cases they try, and the endeavors they pursue inform their subsequent choices and opportunities. I did not set out to specialize in political violence. Through a series of unexpected challenges in the communities I call home, I have been fortunate enough to be part of the response, the understanding, and the healing in the wake of two of the most searing episodes of political violence in our nation's history. I am, in many ways, a reluctant expert in political violence and all it reveals about America.

I led a team that conducted an independent review of the racist riot that occurred in my hometown of Charlottesville, Virginia, on August 12, 2017. Back then, I was a former United States attorney hired by the city government to conduct an after-action report detailing how the city prepared for and managed the Unite the Right (UTR) rally that became a forum in which fascist white nationalists clashed with anti-racist counter-protesters in the small city in which I live. Our team issued a lengthy report that contained harsh criticism of law enforcement, city and state officials, and other decision makers, calling out their failure to protect both public safety and free speech in Charlottesville. The Heaphy Report has become the definitive account of that tragic day.

My experience in Charlottesville ultimately led to my role as chief investigative counsel for the January 6 committee in the House of Representatives. Over the course of my work on these investigations, I have spent considerable time looking closely at these two seminal events. Along with a team of experts, I spent untold hours reviewing footage and reading emails, text messages, and other documents generated before, during, and after by both people who perpetrated and those who tried to prevent them.

Charlottesville and January 6 are inextricably linked in the consciousness of Americans. As horrific as those days were, studying, considering, and talking about them can point us toward a way forward out of the darkness that currently threatens to kill American democracy as we know it.

One central connection between Charlottesville and January 6 is that both events were planned online, in plain view, on social media. The organizers of the Unite the Right rally encouraged like-minded people to attend by actively promoting the event on Facebook, Twitter, Parler, Reddit, and other social media sites. A little more than three years later, the Proud Boys, Oath Keepers, and others who sincerely but misguidedly believed the 2020 presidential election had been stolen used these same platforms to draw attention to the January 6 certification proceeding at the Capitol.

Despite the fact that both the Charlottesville rally and the January 6 attack on the Capitol were planned on open-source channels, law enforcement was woefully unprepared for them. Agencies failed to share information across jurisdictional lines or aggregate information. Implicit racial bias affected preparation for each event, as those agencies failed to appreciate the danger presented by angry white men.

Since the events of January 6, the job of law enforcement has been made more difficult as accountability has been stripped away. In protecting us from future spasms of political violence, law enforcement must work in a new reality, a world in which the president of the United States has pardoned nearly 1,600 people involved in a violent, lethal attack on the US Capitol that aimed to nullify the results of a free and fair election. If investigating, prosecuting, and punishing perpetrators is deterrence, then it logically follows that pardoning acts of political violence and lawlessness will encourage more of the same.

The most salient commonality between Charlottesville and January 6 was how each event metastasized from a focus on one core issue to become a broader forum for the expression of anger at institutions. Charlottesville started as a protest about the removal of Civil War statues in public spaces. It became a protest at which a constellation of groups came together to express anger about how our increasingly diverse culture threatened their historic privilege. The unifying principle on January 6 was belief in the "Big Lie" that the 2020 election had been stolen from President Trump. Many participants in the attack on the Capitol were, however, drawn there by a broader cynicism about government and disbelief in what they routinely hear from politicians, the media, and educational institutions. As in Charlottesville, some January 6 rioters believed that the national government is run by self-interested elites determined to replace them with immigrants. Others were motivated by a belief that public health mandates during the pandemic were baseless and infringed their liberty. These groups came together under a common banner of resistance to a system that they regard as oppressive and believe does not work for them.

The core division in this country revealed by Charlottesville and January 6 prompts both anger and apathy among Americans. While some people express their anger by taking part in mass demonstration events, others simply turn away. Many people in this country don't vote, pay attention to current events, or actively participate in their communities. Withdrawal is as dangerous as anger. A disengaged citizenry is a more insidious threat to democracy, and ultimately more destructive, than a large crowd of angry rioters.

Identifying effective solutions to this division in America will require grassroots involvement by a much wider spectrum of voices than those that currently participate in these discussions. Our future success will require everyone to care and contribute. The best way to restore faith in government is to make it more responsive to the core needs of the people governed. That requires participation and engagement, not apathy and withdrawal. When people of good faith fail to participate, extreme perspectives are amplified and get outsized attention. We need to run toward, not away from, the problems facing this country, those revealed by these episodes of political violence and many others.

"Truth and reconciliation are the only hope for nations that are bitterly divided," Nelson Mandela wrote in 1999.[1] I keep coming back to his words as I think through how we got here, and how to move forward. My hope is that this book helps us understand the meaning of Charlottesville and January 6 so we can learn from them and use those lessons to guide us forward as we, the people, strive to restore civility and defend American democracy, lest we lose it forever.

1

Insider vs. Outsider

From the outside, the violence that took place in Charlottesville in 2017 and at the Capitol on January 6, 2021, looks like manifestations of partisan division. By choosing to call their rally Unite the Right, the racist organizers in Charlottesville purposely classified the event as a conflict of left versus right, appealing to conservatives to band together. The attack on the Capitol had a similarly partisan impetus; in advance of January 6, President Trump told his followers that "radical, leftist Democrats" had stolen the election from him and, by extension, them. At first glance these events seem to suggest that America is a country divided along political lines — red versus blue, left versus right, conservative versus liberal.

After spending time talking with participants on all sides of the conflicts in Charlottesville and at the Capitol, however, I've become convinced that the divide they represent is not left versus right, but rather one between insiders and outsiders. These events each began with a core impetus that attracted attention but then metastasized well beyond the issues that initiated them. What began as a rally to protest the removal of Civil War statues in Charlottesville became a broad forum for people with differing perspectives to express their collective anger at systems they believe are hostile to their interests. The primary motivator for the attack on the Capitol was the widespread fallacy that the election had been stolen. However, people in the crowd that day were also frustrated with systems of governmental control ranging from gun restrictions to COVID masking, vaccine mandates, and diversity programs. Both events became broad forums for expressing anger at the government and other American institutions.

Charlottesville and January 6 reveal that the true division in this country is no longer political, but rather cultural. Americans are less motivated by political ideology than by their faith (or lack thereof) in institutions. The people who showed up to protest in Charlottesville in 2017 and in Washington in 2021 were united in their belief that traditional American systems do not reflect their values, work in support of their welfare, or better their lives. They distrust government, the mainstream media, higher education, and science. They are united more by their cynicism about these pillars of American society than by politics.

2

The Lines of Division

Our political system exacerbates this insider-versus-outsider cultural divide and pushes Americans further apart. We live in "red" states and "blue" states, with policy priorities that widely differ in each. While the California legislature pursues regulation of carbon emissions and the elimination of cash bail, their counterparts in Florida pass laws that ban certain books from public school classrooms, restrict abortion rights, and prevent gender-confirmation surgery. Americans who live in blue states have different levels of taxation, public safety regulation and spending, and restrictions on personal liberty from those who live in red states. In 2021, the year of January 6, "37% of Americans described their political views as moderate, 36% as conservative and 25% as liberal."[1] This political divide is a long-standing feature of American government and is reflected in our representative government, particularly in presidential election years. The Electoral College system created in the Constitution gives each state a certain number of electors corresponding to their number of elected representatives in Congress.[2] The vast majority of electors are from non-competitive states, as most states in the past several election cycles have reliably voted for either a Republican or Democrat for president. As a result, presidential elections are decided by a small number of Americans in swing, or "purple," states. Even within those states, the number of people whose votes could go either way and tip the balance is relatively small.

Divides within our political process reflect deeper disagreement about the efficacy of government. Within the Democratic Party, a large number of voters believe that capitalism is oppressive, is unfair to workers, and perpetuates wealth disparity in America. Bernie Sanders and his Democratic Socialist followers reflect this view. They advocate for the rights of workers, the redistribution of wealth, and the provision of basic services like health care for all Americans. Other Democrats believe that the government should do more to stem the climate crisis and impose a "Green New Deal" of restrictions to protect the planet. These voices clash within the party with more moderate Democrats who share broad policy goals but do not support more fundamental changes to the system proposed by those on the progressive left. This debate within the Democratic Party played out during the 2020 presidential primaries, when President Biden defeated more progressive challengers like Senator Sanders and Senator Elizabeth Warren. The divide continues today with internal policy discussions that require compromise to achieve consensus and implement legislation.

There are similar divisions within the Republican Party, where mainstream conservatives clash with far-right proponents of more radical change. This dynamic played out dramatically in the election of Speaker Kevin McCarthy at the beginning of the 118th Congress, which required 15 rounds of voting among a divided Republican caucus. It continues to manifest in debate over government funding, with members of the Freedom Caucus advocating for more extreme budgetary reductions. These divisions also play out in electoral politics, where some Republicans willing to criticize Donald Trump have consequently been shunned by their own party.

I worked closely with Republican representatives Elizabeth Cheney and Adam Kinzinger on the January 6 select committee and saw firsthand how their principled positions on the attack on the Capitol led to their marginalization and ultimate abandonment by Republican colleagues. Representative Cheney, once the third-ranking Republican in the House of Representatives, lost to a Trump-supported challenger in a primary election. Representative Kinzinger was ostracized by his Republican colleagues and received death threats due to his support for impeachment and his January 6 committee service. Despite their conservative credentials and principled positions on issues like abortion, immigration, foreign policy, and the size of the federal budget, Representatives Cheney and Kinzinger were no longer welcome in the Republican caucus. As with the Democrats, disagreements among Republicans complicate any efforts to establish where the fault lines exist in American politics, let alone draw simple conclusions about the left/right divide.

These intra-party disputes do, however, provide more evidence of the insider-versus-outsider division in America. With both parties, tensions exist and conflicts arise largely between institutionalists who believe in incremental change and those who want more immediate, fundamental change. Far-left Democratic Socialists and far-right members of the Freedom Caucus arguably have much in common in this regard: They believe the traditional system of government is broken and needs radical reform. While they disagree on what specific changes should be made, they stand in opposition to traditional elements within their own parties.

3

Information Silos

Another manifestation of core division in America is the way in which we consume information. Many commentators have bemoaned the fact that the manner in which Americans receive news has become remarkably siloed. We can't agree on basic facts surrounding important issues because we aren't viewing the same news and opinions — not even close. This development both reflects and reinforces the division between those who want to rely on and support institutions and those who reject them. While Republicans watch Fox News and read the *Wall Street Journal*, Democrats tune in to MS NOW (formerly MSNBC) and read the *New York Times*. In the stories they highlight and the opinions they present, many conservative sites focus on the alleged weaponization of the criminal justice system against President Trump in the years leading up to his second term, the perceived dangers of diversity programming, and skepticism about the impact of climate change. Liberal sites have a fundamentally different view of these same issues and call for increased accountability in the criminal justice system, proactive measures to promote equity and inclusion, and sounding the alarm about the dangers of climate change.

These contrasting sources of information do not simply present differing views on policies. They thematically reinforce a broad perspective about the efficacy of systems. Liberal outlets urge the government to use its authority to make the world more just and productive, while conservative outlets promote the traditional view that the government's social justice and economic initiatives are fraught with unintended consequences and often misguided. They even darkly suggested for many years that US governmental authority was tyrannical. With President Trump's 2024 reelection and the rapid implementation of policies and practices outlined in Project 2025, a blueprint for governance that was spearheaded by the conservative Heritage Foundation, the tables have turned, with traditionally liberal outlets now warning against autocracy.

These news and opinion sites subtly or explicitly suggest winners and losers, what's right and what's wrong. This is intentional, as it allows each source to gain market share by appealing to people who share its perspective. These approaches might reflect and cater to divergent worldviews, but they are also, perhaps primarily, business models. The media landscape is highly competitive, with more and more outlets vying for the attention of consumers of information. News is also more nationalized, as newspapers and television networks in small communities increasingly disappear or reduce costs. As a result, the old saw "All politics is local" has been turned on its head. Now it seems all politics is national. As a result, more Americans get their news from sources that reinforce rather than challenge their perspective on important issues, which furthers our tribal divisions and ideological separations.

I find myself falling prey to this pattern of siloed consumption of information that reinforces my perspective. While driving to work, I listen to NPR, which, along with PBS, lost all of its federal funding in the first year of President Trump's second term. I read the *Times* and the *Washington Post* every day, and I watch and am sometimes invited to appear on cable news — MS NOW and CNN, never Fox News. I understand that the choices I make reflect a value system. I believe those sources emphasize reliable facts and circumstances and strive to uphold journalistic ethics. I don't often lift my head from those sources to evaluate news coverage from different perspectives. The result is a circular feedback loop — what I read reinforces my views, which makes me read those same sources and strengthens those views.

Higher education is another institution that is riven by division. Colleges and universities have been at the forefront of efforts to prioritize equity and inclusion for decades, and they have created new areas of research and scholarship that extend beyond traditional definitions of academic rigor. Administrators have attempted to create communities that celebrate diversity and reflect the pluralistic student bodies on their campuses. Critics of higher education have suggested that this effort has evolved in ways somehow hostile to certain groups, whether they be white students, conservatives, Jewish students, or others. They point to a woke culture that promotes self-censorship by discouraging the expression of "incorrect" points of view, undermining constructive discourse on campus and diminishing the value of the educational experience for all students. To these observers, higher education is broken. They believe college no longer creates a path toward knowledge and prosperity but rather arbitrarily indoctrinates students into a culture of enforced liberalism. In his second term, President

Trump has used the power of the federal government to target institutions of higher education and aggressively end many of these practices and policies.

This divergence of opinion about colleges and universities is another manifestation of the core American divide of insiders versus outsiders. Our differing understandings of higher education go beyond policy disputes and become more about the efficacy of the institution, broadly speaking. While some people continue to see colleges as places that advance knowledge and create opportunity, others see them as indoctrination machines that promote beliefs at odds with traditional American values. The core divide has been belief in the institution of American higher education versus cynicism about its direction, rather than liberal versus conservative beliefs.

We have also seen the divide of insider versus outsider in Americans' differing views on scientific issues like COVID-19 and climate change. The pandemic fundamentally altered life in America like few events in the nation's history. It created a host of challenges for government at all levels and required the unprecedented regulation of our daily lives to prevent even more widespread death and illness. Closures of schools and businesses, compulsory masking and social distancing, and ultimately vaccine mandates all stemmed from scientific decisions designed to protect public health. Decision makers responsible for these rules relied on experts to provide advice about a new virus, without reliable long-term understanding of the threat it posed.

Americans had widely divergent responses to COVID restrictions and public health measures imposed during the pandemic. While the weight of scientific opinion supported the efficacy of public health mandates for measures such as masking, social distancing, and vaccination, there were contrasting voices that resisted restrictions and gave credence to social media and political messaging not supported by data or public health officials. One of the loudest skeptical voices was that of Robert F. Kennedy Jr., who has no medical or scientific training and yet was named by President Trump in his second term to be his secretary of health and human services. While some believed Dr. Anthony Fauci, who served as the director of the National Institute of Allergy and Infectious Diseases from 1984 to 2022, and their local public health officials, others speculated about the motives and trustworthiness of the government, pharmaceutical companies, the liberal media, even powerful private-sector individuals like Bill Gates who were trying to help.

What could have been a global event that reinforced our shared humanity became another manifestation of our core division. Our bodies' biological responses to the virus were agnostic to the opinions we held about it. Responsible studies have found that hundreds of thousands fewer people would have died from COVID had there not been so much hesitancy around commonsense public health measures.[1] The science wasn't seriously in dispute. Lack of belief in that science stemmed from distrust of the messengers. Cynicism about the system prevailed over facts and scientific inquiry.

Climate change is another area where the scientific community and its standards have been disputed and even rejected. There can be little doubt that greenhouse gas emissions have affected the earth's climate and threaten the health and safety of people around the world. Despite there being a clear scientific consensus, some point to snowstorms as evidence that the planet is not warming and suggest that changes in global temperatures are cyclical. One result of such skepticism is to elevate entrenched economic interests over long-term health of the planet, favoring fossil fuel extraction and consumption, for instance, over the development of alternative sources of energy. As with the pandemic, climate change skeptics do not trust the messenger and question the motivation of those who are sounding the alarm.

The divisions that are revealed in how we consume information, how we view higher education, and how we respond to scientific findings also appear in our perception of the events in Charlottesville and at the Capitol — and all point to a core division in America between those who believe in institutions and those who distrust them. The participants in the UTR rally and the rioters at the Capitol were united in anger at the government and other institutions they believe do not protect their interests.

If we are to remedy this core divide, we must accurately assess it. While political polarization is undoubtedly a pressing issue, it does not alone explain the sharp divides that erupted in violence in Charlottesville and at the Capitol. Our divided politics is a symptom of this core dynamic, not a cause. Americans don't disagree because they are Democrats and Republicans, but rather because some trust in the traditional systems of information, education, and control and some do not.

4

"There Is No Cavalry Coming"

Soon after President Trump won enough delegates to secure the 2024 Republican nomination, former attorney general Eric Holder reacted to that news on X (formerly known as Twitter) by posting the following message: "There is no cavalry coming. No miracle solution. No saviors. In the end, we, the American people — not any of our institutions — have to save our democracy by voting in defense of that democracy this fall. We are the cavalry. The responsibility is ours."[1]

Holder's words were meant as a wake-up call to Americans who had assumed that the former president's attempt to return to the White House would be stopped — by Republican primary voters, aggressive reporting, criminal courts, the Constitution, or some other "savior." He wanted to disabuse those people of the false hope that our institutions operate as independent guardrails to prevent a dangerous outcome and protect democracy.

As I read the attorney general's words, it occurred to me that they apply to a much broader conflict in

America than just the 2024 presidential election. The issues that informed the political violence in Charlottesville in 2017 and at the Capitol on January 6, 2021, and the resulting division they reveal will not be remedied by any one politician or other savior. In particular, our current system of government at all levels is not equipped to bring Americans together and diminish the division that roils our nation. Rather than constructively address the pressing issues facing our democracy, our current system protects incumbency, discourages compromise, and reinforces the cynicism described above. Gerrymandered districts diminish true competition. Unlimited campaign spending protects special interests. The result is ineffective government that reinforces skepticism and exacerbates the political and cultural differences between Americans. As Holder observed, the institutions of our federal, state, and local governments are not equipped to reduce division, heal America, and protect democracy.

President Trump was, of course, victorious, and the aggressiveness with which he has sought to obliterate norms, seize power for the executive, and subvert the rule of law have been breathtaking. The threats we now face are bigger than any one politician, and our deep division will remain regardless of who prevails in the next midterms or presidential election. Given that persistent reality, we need to turn to organic solutions that promote constructive dialogue, encourage community and common purpose, and unite Americans around a common set of values. This cannot be done by relying on elected and appointed government officials to step into the breach personally or to enforce guardrails through the courts or law enforcement agencies, but rather must be achieved by regular people exerting a collective will in favor of fairness and democratic processes over partisan outcomes. "We are the cavalry. The responsibility is ours."

5

"Do the Right Thing"

From the time I was a young lawyer, Eric Holder has been a role model and inspiration to me. In the fall of 1993, Holder was the newly appointed United States attorney for the District of Columbia. He stepped into that position at a time when the crime rate in Washington, DC, was on a disturbing increase. Crack cocaine had been introduced into DC and other urban communities just a few years before, which fueled competition among drug sellers that was often enforced with gun violence.[1] According to a 2002 National Drug Intelligence Center threat assessment, "The District had more drug treatment admissions to publicly funded facilities for cocaine abuse than for any other drug from 1994 through 1999, and that number increased approximately 510 percent from 363 in 1996 to 2,225 in 1999."[2] The situation became so untenable that the mayor of Washington, DC, Sharon Pratt Kelly, asked President Clinton to deploy the National Guard on the streets of Washington to augment the resources of local law enforcement.[3] While the president did not accommodate her request, he did authorize the hiring of new assistant United States attorneys (AUSAs) to help increase the pace of criminal prosecutions.

Unlike other American cities, because of its unique position as a federal territory rather than a state, Washington, DC, has no local district attorney. The US attorney and their assistants are charged with investigating all crimes that occur in the city and prosecuting criminal violations in both local and federal courts. The US attorney functions as both the local and federal prosecutor, a status unique among federal districts around the country.

Eric Holder's primary responsibility when he became US attorney was to hire these new AUSAs and deploy them as part of a strategy to combat the surge in violence. I was fortunate enough to be one of the first new prosecutors he hired. US Attorney Holder swore me in as an assistant United States attorney on April 25, 1994. After administering the oath of office and saying hello to my wife, he led me into his spacious corner office at 555 Fourth Street NW, just a block away from both the DC and federal courthouses. He told me that he did not have a long list of rules that I must follow as I approached my new responsibilities as a prosecutor. He explained, however, that as an AUSA I would have immense discretion to make decisions that directly and significantly affected the lives of many people and that there was one rule that I must heed at all times: "Do the right thing." He encouraged me to always follow my core sense of justice and belief in what is right. He said that the right thing might not always be the most aggressive from a prosecutorial standpoint and that it would sometimes result in disappointment among those with whom I worked. He told me that he had hired me because he believed in my ability to be fair, to exercise good judgment, and to do justice.

I have recalled that advice from my first day on the job many times throughout my career. Holder was correct that doing the right thing sometimes led me to say no to agents or victims if I had misgivings about how evidence had been obtained or otherwise believed we couldn't prove a case. Sometimes the most important tests of a prosecutor's judgment are reflected in decisions *not* to pursue cases. I would come to learn that the right thing is often reduced to telling the truth, even when that truth is unpopular and difficult to hear.

Almost fifteen years after that afternoon on US Attorney Holder's couch, we ended up working together again at the Department of Justice. On February 3, 2009, Holder was appointed attorney general of the United States.[4] Several months later, President Obama nominated me to serve as United States attorney for the Western District of Virginia, and I was confirmed by the Senate. I approached the privilege of serving as US attorney with the example Eric Holder had set for me in mind and tried to emulate his priorities, his judgment, and his leadership in my own district. I gave every AUSA whom I hired the same instruction I'd received: "Do the right thing."

Sometime in 2010, a group of newly confirmed US attorneys was invited to the White House for a brief meeting with the man who had appointed us all — President Barack Obama. We assembled in the ornate East Room of the White House and waited for the president to greet us. He walked into the room with the attorney general by his side and proceeded to give us advice very similar to what Holder had told me years before: "You're not my lawyers, you're the people's lawyers." The president told us that he did not want us to make decisions with a view toward what would benefit the administration or forward any political agenda. Rather, he instructed us, we should at all times make decisions and set priorities based on our belief in what is best for the people of our districts.

He reminded us that doing the right thing meant separating politics from justice. AG Holder looked on, nodding in agreement as the president reinforced our independence.

I was reminded of both of these events at the outset of my work on the January 6 committee, and especially during my first meeting with committee chairman Bennie Thompson. During that initial conversation, Chairman Thompson told me that he was familiar with my work as a US attorney and with the report I had authored in the wake of the Charlottesville events in 2017. He said that he wanted me to pursue the January 6 investigation in a similar fashion — gathering the facts and telling the truth about what happened. Specifically, Chairman Thompson explained that he wanted this investigation to "follow the facts, wherever they lead." I believe I told him about Eric Holder's advice to me as a young AUSA and assured him that I would pursue our important work with that same commitment to doing the right thing.

The ideals expressed by these three men — Eric Holder, Barack Obama, and Bennie Thompson — embody the very best of government. They all inspired me to be guided by facts and evidence, not politics. They encouraged me to tell the truth, no matter how inconvenient that truth might be. They prioritized ethical behavior and a commitment to fairness over convictions or predetermined outcomes. They appealed to my core sense of what is right and wrong and identified that ideal of justice as the necessary foundation of my personal commitment to be part of the "cavalry" of protecting democracy.

Ironically, my career led me to focus on moments when others in government did not do the right thing and instead failed spectacularly to protect democracy. Our investigations of both the Charlottesville events and the January 6 attack on the Capitol described dysfunctional government. Both investigations include sharp criticisms of governmental officials at all levels who fell well short of the high standards of professionalism and justice described above. These leaders acted out of self-interest and failed to meet the moment. The system didn't work in Charlottesville or at the Capitol. To the contrary, these events will go down in history as colossal failures of government.

6

Polarized Politics

The imperative of individual responsibility to protect democracy is made more urgent by the inability of our current system of representative government to heal itself. Our current system protects incumbency and discourages compromise in several significant ways. The result is a representative government that reflects the core divisions within America as opposed to our common interests and values, and that fails to address the pressing issues of the day. This dysfunction in turn reinforces the public's cynicism about government and increases the sense of an insider-versus-outsider division.

Under our constitutional system, the conduct of elections is a power reserved for the states. Article I, Section 4, of the Constitution provides that "the Times, Places and Manner of holding Elections for Senators and Representatives, shall be prescribed in each State by the Legislature thereof." Pursuant to this provision, state legislatures conduct elections for both federal and state offices. They set the rules that govern elections in each state and have ultimate legal authority over the results.

One facet of the states' power to conduct elections is the drawing of legislative districts. Under Article I, Section 2, of the Constitution, representatives "shall be apportioned among the several States . . . according to their respective numbers" and revised every ten years. The state legislatures control the process of drawing the lines that govern their representatives in Congress, as well as their own state legislative districts. These legislative processes typically result in revised district maps every ten years, incorporating data from the most recent US Census. Legislators evaluate population growth or decline, changing demographics, and other census data to reconsider the number and nature of individual districts within each state. State legislators may delegate the authority to draw these lines to others, though in most states the legislature retains ultimate authority to accept district lines and control the redistricting process.[1] In addition to census data, the legislators consider existing districts, including the current representatives who occupy those districts and how they may be affected by changes to the lines. Some districts must be redrawn in ways that change the number of legislators apportioned to each state. According to the Constitution, each state will have at least 1 representative, and then an apportionment calculation divides the remaining 385 seats among the states. Congress has power over the method used to calculate apportionment.[2]

Because the process of redistricting is controlled by politicians with direct and personal interests in the outcome of the process, it is no surprise that it broadly protects incumbency. The vast majority of legislative districts in Congress and in state legislatures are designed to achieve a predetermined ratio of party control. This phenomenon is called gerrymandering, a term that harks back to 1812 when the Massachusetts legislature redrew state senate districts to favor the party led by Governor Elbridge Gerry.[3] The word has come to refer to the partisan manipulation of geographic boundaries that define districts for elected representatives.

Gerrymandering reflects a clear partisan lean and results across the country in districts made up largely of either Democratic or Republican residents. The maps drawn or approved by legislators reflect the approximate ratio of party control in each state. If the Republicans control the state legislature, they will supervise a redistricting process that reinforces that control. Democrats similarly protect their interests when they control state legislatures. They do this by drawing districts that are designed to be "safe" for one party or the other, rather than being truly competitive. The legislators who draw the maps sometimes go to extremes, producing districts that seem illogical and disjointed. This process has been particularly politicized since President Trump's reelection, as both red and blue state legislatures have sought to redraw district lines to create more seats for the majority party and influence the overall balance of power in a closely divided House of Representatives.

According to the Princeton Gerrymandering Project, thirteen of the fifty states fail a redistricting report card designed to reflect whether each district is fairly and equally distributed based on metrics of partisan fairness, geographic features, partisan composition, and minority composition.[4] And according to a 2023 study by Harvard researchers published in the *Proceedings of the National Academy of Sciences*, the 2020 redistricting led to more so-called safe seats that protect incumbents. "Gerrymandering does end up reducing electoral competition," researcher Kosuke Imai said. "As a result, there are a lot more incumbents being elected. And electoral outcomes tend to be less close than the predicted margins."[5] The result is very little true competition in the vast majority of elections for Congress and state legislators — the legislative bodies designed by our founders to most directly reflect the views of the voting public.

As each district is gerrymandered to reflect population data that ensures the control of one party or the other, there is little chance of an upset or a particular district changing from one party to the other. Republican districts stay Republican, and Democratic districts repeatedly send Democrats to Congress and the state legislature. At both the state and federal levels, districts that flip from one party to the other are exceedingly rare. According to the Brennan Center for Justice in 2022, "There are now fewer competitive districts than at any point in the last 52 years." After the most recent redistricting cycle, "we saw the percentage of competitive congressional districts fall even further to just 14 percent."[6]

The fact that legislative districts are reliably within the control of one party or the other pushes our politics to the extreme. The strongest threat to reelection faced by members of Congress typically comes from within their own party. The most likely way a member of Congress in a safe district will lose is if they are outflanked to the extreme by a primary challenger.

The district in which I live reflects this phenomenon. The Fifth District of Virginia has for years been drawn as a safe Republican district. While the district includes the liberal college town of Charlottesville, the vast majority of it is rural and conservative. The Fifth District has been represented by Republican members of Congress consistently since 2010. In 2018, Republican Denver Riggleman was elected to represent the Fifth District. Riggleman was a libertarian who believed in limited government. Consistent with the philosophy that government should not restrict personal choice or limit individual freedom, he was a supporter of gay marriage. In 2020, Riggleman officiated at the wedding of two gay men who had been volunteers in his campaign. Later that year, Bob Good, a self-described "Biblical conservative" who cited Riggleman's support for gay marriage as the impetus for his campaign, defeated Riggleman in the Republican primary. The Democratic candidate in the Fifth District in 2020 was Charlottesville resident Dr. Cameron Webb, a Black physician with both law and medical degrees. Webb supported gay marriage and other progressive policies and had strong support in Charlottesville. Nonetheless, Good resoundingly defeated Webb by approximately twenty thousand votes. Despite his credentials and strong, well-funded campaign, Webb had almost no chance to win due to the demographic composition of the Fifth District.

The protection of incumbency reflected in our gerrymandered redistricting process has the practical effect of discouraging compromise. If a member of Congress or a state legislator can only lose to a more extreme candidate within his or her own party, that legislator has little incentive to work with members of the other party. The threat of a primary challenge pushes elected officials in both parties toward more partisan positions. Rather than working toward compromise solutions to difficult problems, members of legislative bodies retreat to their respective partisan positions and demonize their opponents. Compromise is actually risky, as it opens up members on both sides to a potential challenge from a more partisan candidate within their own party.

The refusal to compromise or work toward bipartisan solutions fueled by gerrymandered districts has led to paralysis in government. So many important issues are mired in this partisan divide, which results in no meaningful change in policy. Politicians and policymakers across the ideological divide agree that we need to do more to fix an immigration system that is underfunded and ineffective. Nonetheless, Congress has been unable to pass legislation to address clear problems. Similarly, voters in both parties believe that gun violence is an issue that needs to be addressed, but the two parties' official positions on access to firearms prevent meaningful reform. While we often agree on what problems need to be remedied, we disagree so strongly on possible solutions that legislators hold fast to core partisan positions to protect their political flanks rather than engage with goodwill in a give-and-take process.

7

Increasing Competition, Encouraging Compromise

There are several steps we could take to diminish the polarization that infects our current politics. One obvious way to make government more effective would be the creation of a system that encourages rather than eliminates true political competition. Instead of designing districts to protect incumbents, we could draw them to consistently reflect geographic and community boundaries, contiguous areas that share common features, rather than artificial groupings designed to ensure partisan control. A more objective approach to drawing lines based purely on census data would result in districts that may vacillate between Republican and Democratic control over time. The officials elected in these less partisan districts would have much more incentive to compromise and work with counterparts across the aisle.

To minimize the risk of political considerations influencing the redistricting process, we should remove legislators from the granular work of drawing district boundaries. Consistent with their Article I power to manage elections, state legislatures could delegate the authority to draw district lines to outside experts — judges, citizen panels, or academics. Some states have done just this, creating nonpartisan redistricting commissions or other processes designed to minimize the effect of politics on this crucial process. Most states that have done this also ban commissioners from running for office in the districts they draw. Others ban legislative staff and/or lobbyists from serving on the commissions.[1]

In November 2008, California voters passed the Voters FIRST Act, authorizing the creation of the California Citizens Redistricting Commission to draw new district lines, taking the job out of the hands of the California State Legislature and transferring it to the citizens. According to the commission's website, "The Commission must draw the district lines in conformity with strict, nonpartisan rules designed to create districts of relatively equal population that will provide fair representation for all Californians." It is made up of five Republicans, five Democrats, and four unaffiliated members, chosen through a lengthy process involving public applications and a lottery.[2]

California is one of nine states (in addition to Alaska, Arizona, Colorado, Idaho, Michigan, Montana, New

York, and Washington) whose state legislature has no ultimate control over the redistricting outcome. Other states, like Virginia, have redistricting commissions but have not bestowed them with complete independence. Rather, the commissions send proposals to the state legislature for approval.[3] According to the American Bar Association, "The record of redistricting commissions has been mixed, with some succeeding in drafting and implementing plans and others failing. Looking at the national landscape, commissions have failed for numerous reasons, while functional commissions have all shared the same qualities." Those qualities include a tie-breaker vote in case of a Democrat and Republican draw on any decisions, non-politically-appointed members, and, importantly, final and ultimate control over the district lines. "As Washington, D.C., and individual states look toward reforming the redistricting process," the ABA writes, "they should keep these lessons in mind."[4]

The ABA designates the commissions in California, Colorado, and Michigan as "Gold Standard" commissions from which other states can learn. They have received positive feedback on redistricting efforts and share the qualities of independent non-politically-appointed commissioners and the power to actually implement the lines they choose, not having to defer to their state legislatures.[5]

For many years, there has been a national effort to require independent redistricting commissions for all states. The effort was included in the omnibus election integrity bill called the For the People Act, which passed the House in 2019 during the 116th Congress but was not given a vote in the Senate. The bill was reintroduced at the beginning of the 117th Congress as HR 1 and S 1. This bill would have required each state to have a fully independent fifteen-member redistricting commission composed of five Republicans, five Democrats, and five independents. Dispite its inclusion of numerous other reforms to the election process, it did not have enough support to pass.[6]

Another way to push back against the deleterious effects of partisan gerrymandering is the use of ranked choice (RCV) and top-two voting processes, both of which diminish the importance of party affiliation by eliminating separate primaries for the major parties. With RCV, all candidates and voters are eligible to participate in a single primary election. Voters rank their first, second, and third choices for each office. If one candidate is ranked first on a majority of ballots, they are declared the winner. But if no candidate receives a majority of first-choice ballots, then the candidate with the lowest number of votes is eliminated and that person's ballots are distributed to the remaining candidates. This process continues until one candidate has received a majority of voters' first, second, or third votes. California, Maine, and Alaska use RCV systems to select congressional and state legislative candidates, and some jurisdictions around the country use RCV for local elections. All told, as of the 2022 election, ranked choice voting was used in sixty-two jurisdictions, ranging from Alaska and Maine to New York City and Cambridge, Massachusetts.[7]

Primary elections are similarly nonpartisan in a top-two election system. In states that use this process, the two candidates who receive the most votes in the nonpartisan primary election advance to a runoff in the general election, regardless of their party affiliation. The general election may have two Republican or two Democratic candidates in a particular district, depending upon the results of the primary. California, Nebraska, and Washington used a top-two primary system as of September 2023, while Alaska and Louisiana used a variation on the format.[8]

By diminishing party control of primary elections, ranked choice and top-two voting systems give voters a wider array of choices in elections even within gerrymandered districts. In a primarily Democratic district, there could be a ranked choice contest between a Democrat who favors compromise with Republicans and another Democrat who favors a more absolutist approach to particular problems. All voters, not simply Democrats, would have the chance to vote for these candidates and weigh in on the relative utility of each approach. These nonpartisan systems give more voters power to influence elections and ultimately choose candidates who more closely reflect their positions. Legislators are therefore more directly accountable to all of the constituents they represent, creating incentives to address rather than avoid important and complicated issues.

Both ranked choice voting and top-two systems lead to measurably positive results on metrics ranging from voter satisfaction to increased incentive to compromise among candidates. For example, voters in states that routinely use RCV report overwhelming satisfaction with the system in surveys.[9] According to a 2020 study in the Minneapolis–St. Paul area, implementing RCV in 2009 and 2013 caused a 10 percent increase in voter turnout, and even greater increases for precincts with higher poverty rates.[10] Turnout rates have continued to climb, all the way to a stunning 54 percent participation of eligible voters in a 2021 municipal election. "It's a pretty phenomenal turnout . . . Every voter felt like their vote counted, and indeed it did," Jeanne Massey, executive director of the pro-RCV organization FairVote Minnesota, was quoted as saying in the *Minneapolis Star Tribune*.[11] A different study in 2021 found especially high turnout rates among younger voters in RCV cities, which the researchers were able to attribute to "great campaign civility," another common, measurable result of implementing RCV voting.[12] "Findings suggest RCV acts as a positive mobilizing force for youth voting through increasing campaign contact," the research summarized.[13]

Research also suggests top-two primary systems can even result in more moderate candidates entering a race. Christian Grose, academic director of the USC Schwarzenegger Institute for State and Global Policy, compared election results of US House of Representatives members in the three states that have a top-two primary system: California, Louisiana, and Washington. He also examined any effect on those states' legislative races. Interestingly, Grose examined the lawmakers' votes over fifteen years to examine the effect over time. He found that "the top-two primary led to less extreme behavior by members of Congress in the three open primary states."[14] He explained further in a 2020 research article that "legislators elected in the top-two primary system are more moderate than those elected in closed primary systems," in part because "the threat of a same-party general leads legislators to moderate as they may face a same-party general election challenge in the future."[15]

8

Money in Politics

Another key factor that protects incumbents and diminishes compromise in government is money. There are few meaningful limits on campaign donations in our political system, which results in substantial sums of money flowing to candidates for office. Incumbents receive the large majority of these contributions, most of which are given by corporations, unions, or groups with a vested interest in particular issues. Together with gerrymandered districts, the steady stream of campaign dollars protects incumbents and diminishes compromise and competition.

In two seminal cases, the United States Supreme Court has ruled that spending on campaigns is a form of free speech protected by the First Amendment. In 1976, the court ruled in *Buckley v. Valeo* that campaign contributions are a form of expression protected by the First Amendment. Accordingly, any restriction upon the fundamental right of free expression would be subject to "strict scrutiny" and must be justified by a "compelling governmental interest."[1] The court essentially applied a balancing test — evaluating whether restrictions on political spending were justified by the interest such limits were designed to protect. The opinion described that public interest as "encouraging citizen participation in political campaigns while continuing to guard against the corrupting potential of large financial contributions to candidates." Applying strict scrutiny, the court in *Buckley* overruled an overall cap on spending by candidates for federal office and their campaign committees. This ruling ensures that candidates for federal offices and independent advocacy groups can spend unlimited amounts to support campaigns, without restriction. The court also ruled that candidates can spend an unlimited amount of personal funds on campaigns.

In 2010, the court again recognized campaign spending as protected speech in *Citizens United v. Federal Elections Commission.*[2] In *Citizens United*, the court considered the constitutionality of a complete federal ban on campaign contributions by corporations or labor unions. That ban was based on two distinct policy benefits. First, a ban on corporate campaign spending prevented the "corrosive and distorting effects of immense accumulations of wealth that are accumulated with the help of the corporate form."

Second, the law had an anti-corruption rationale, designed to prevent expenditures being given as quid pro quo for commitments from candidates.[3] The court rejected both policy rationales and invalidated the prohibition on corporate giving. Again applying strict scrutiny, the court found that the policy interests supporting the ban were insufficient to overcome the free speech rights of corporations and unions.

Since the Supreme Court invalidated limitations on spending by corporations, nonprofit political action committees have been incorporated to solicit money to support an array of causes and facilitate unlimited spending on campaigns. Section 501(c)(4) of the Internal Revenue Code makes contributions to social welfare organizations tax-deductible, which further incentivizes contributions to these nonprofit corporations. These special interest groups are colloquially known as Super PACS. They cannot legally coordinate with campaigns, as such coordination would violate FEC regulations that survived *Citizens United*. They are, however, free to purchase television advertising, engage in direct mail and door-to-door advocacy, and provide additional support to candidates for office. Unlike official campaign organizations, they need not disclose their donors to the FEC, which allows contributors to these issue advocacy groups to remain anonymous.

Since *Citizens United* was decided in 2010, there is virtually no restriction on the ability of individuals and special interest organizations to support political campaigns. Wealthy donors are able to pour unlimited amounts of money into Super PACs, which funnel that money into advocacy efforts on behalf of particular candidates who support particular issues. Though these efforts must officially be disconnected from campaigns, that separation is difficult to police and enforce. Mitt Romney came under fire at a presidential debate in 2012 for calling a Super PAC that supported him "my Super PAC."[4] He later had to walk back the comments, promising, "I haven't spoken with any of the people that are involved with my super PAC in months."[5] Hillary Clinton also came under fire for large Super PAC donations in the 2016 campaign and had to defend against allegations of involvement at a presidential debate, saying, "It is not my PAC."[6]

Stephen Colbert famously made a mockery of this aspect of Super PAC law by creating his own, real Super PAC in 2011 called Americans for a Better Tomorrow, Tomorrow. The FEC even signed off on it as a legitimate Super PAC. The group raised $1.2 million by early 2012 and supported real political candidates in the Iowa and South Carolina presidential primaries, an effort that included outrageous commercials and public statements. The bit revealed the loopholes — which Colbert called "loop-chasms" — in how campaign finance laws operate, ultimately winning the comedian one of the highest honors in journalism, the Peabody Award.[7]

The nonprofit group OpenSecrets is a nonpartisan research organization that tracks campaign spending. OpenSecrets estimates that in the election immediately following *Citizens United*, campaign spending by 501(c)(4) Super PACs increased by 53 percent from the previous election cycle.[8] In 2020, Super PACs spent a record $3,427,543,995 to support federal election campaigns. The vast majority of the money raised and spent by Super PACs goes to support incumbents. In the 2022 election cycle, the top fifty recipients of Super PAC donations in Congress were all incumbents, ranging from Republican representative Cathy McMorris Rogers, who received $3,344,596, to Democratic representative Pete Aguilar, who received $1,446,952.[9]

Super PACs invest their campaign spending in candidates whose votes in Congress demonstrate support for the special interests they were created to advance.

The Club for Growth is a conservative organization that supports "reducing income tax rates and repealing the death tax . . . the full repeal of Obamacare . . . regulatory reform and deregulation . . . and expanding school choice."[10] In 2022, the Club for Growth spent $69,864,090 on political campaigns through various Super PACs and other organizations it controls.[11] The vast majority of this spending went to support incumbent Republicans who champion those issues. Similarly, the League of Conservation Voters Victory Fund promotes environmental stewardship and the mitigation of climate change. The LCV Victory Fund spent $33,303,633 on political contributions in 2022, all of which went to support incumbent Democratic candidates or to oppose Republicans.[12]

Their ability to spend unlimited amounts of money on campaigns gives Super PACs enormous influence over our politics. Members of Congress run for office every two years. They are incessantly raising money to ensure they have the resources to fund their never-ending campaigns for reelection. These members understand that access to the tremendous sums of money provided by special interest groups is dependent on supporting particular policies favored by the Super PACs. As a result, they have a disincentive to compromise with members who oppose those policies — the almost certain loss of financial support from Super PACs. Republicans have little incentive to work with Democrats on commonsense restrictions on access to firearms, as they risk losing the support of the National Rifle Association and other pro-gun groups that provide millions of dollars to Republicans through Super PACs. Similarly, Democrats are reluctant to work with Republicans on regulatory reform as they risk losing the support of well-funded labor unions who spend millions supporting pro-union Democrats via Super PACs. Money in politics perpetuates gridlock and discourages members from compromise solutions, as any perceived retreat from absolute support for a particular position jeopardizes the special interest money that funds campaigns. Coupled with gerrymandering, money in politics paralyzes our legislatures and makes it much more difficult to achieve results, which then fuels the skepticism in government described above.

The undue influence of money in politics is not a partisan issue. Republicans and Democrats have benefited from the Supreme Court's ruling in *Citizens United* and now greedily solicit and receive large contributions from Super PACs. According to OpenSecrets, outside organizations spent $1,266,011,505 on "conservative" candidates and causes — about 55 percent of the total Super PAC and outside group spending in that cycle. Other organizations spent $935,436,195 on "liberal" candidates and causes, about 40 percent of the total.[13] This data shows that both parties have adjusted to this Wild West of campaign finance and benefit from the lack of regulation on spending.

9

Evening the Campaign Finance Playing Field

Remedies to the outsized influence of money on our politics are hard to identify given the Supreme Court recognition of political contributions as a form of protected speech. However, some innovative solutions are being implemented primarily at the state and local levels. While the court has ruled that the Constitution forbids a total ban or undue restrictions on political contributions, some states provide public funds to offset those from Super PACs and outside donors. For example, Connecticut, Arizona, and Maine offer full public financing for candidates for both legislative and statewide offices.[1] State laws provide public funding for candidates who reach a particular threshold of support, as reflected in primary votes, contributions, or other metrics. The Connecticut law enhances public support for candidates in "party-dominant" districts, an incentive designed to counter the effect of gerrymandering.[2]

Minnesota has been offering some level of public

financing for candidates since 1974, an initiative that was a response to the Watergate scandal and what it revealed about the corrosive impact of fundraising on electoral politics. The state has a two-part system composed of direct public subsidy payments and a political contribution refund program. Put simply, candidates for statewide office can get partial grants if they agree to spending limits, and then the donors can have up to 50 percent of their contribution refunded by the state.[3]

In addition to public funding programs, both Connecticut and South Carolina restrict the campaign finance activities of lobbyists. South Carolina limits registered lobbyists from donating to any candidate for a body the lobbyist has previously lobbied. A lobbyist also can't host fundraisers or ask for campaign contributions from others. In Connecticut, lobbyists can only donate up to $100 to the campaigns of candidates for most offices, and likewise cannot host fundraisers or act as a "bundler" for donations.[4]

Programs in other states focus on regulating coordination between donor entities and candidates, including one in California that widens the definition of *coordination* to include a litany of activities. For example, a donation is illegal "if it is made at the request, suggestion, or direction of, or in cooperation, arrangement, consultation, concert or coordination with the candidate or if the candidate participated in making any decision or had any discussions with the creator, producer, or distributor of the communication, the person paying for that communication, regarding the content, timing, location, mode, intended audience, volume of distribution, frequency of placing the communication." In other words, as the Campaign Legal Center puts it, it limits the kind of wink-and-nod coordination that usually flies under the radar.[5]

Other novel programs include what New York City calls its matching funds program. Since 1988, candidates for city offices have been able to agree to campaign spending limits and increased financial oversight in exchange for six-to-one matching funds for every dollar raised by small donors (under $175).[6] As the Brennan Center for Justice writes of the program, "By pumping up the value of small contributions, the New York City system gives [candidates] an incentive to reach out to their own constituents rather than focusing all their attention on wealthy out-of-district donors, leading them to attract more diverse donors into the political process. This is markedly different, they explained, from how they and other candidates conduct campaigns at the state level."[7] This allows challengers and candidates who do not benefit from Super PAC contributions to compete financially with more generously funded incumbents. The small-donor matching fund does not violate *Citizens United* or otherwise restrict the ability of special interest groups to influence elections. It does, however, provide somewhat of an offset to special interest money. A bill to enact small-donor matching funding has been introduced in Congress, though it faces little prospect of success given the lack of zeal by either party to change the current system.

The City of Seattle has developed a novel program that provides "democracy vouchers" to city residents, who can use those vouchers to provide support to candidates for local office, and the city council has allocated $3 million to it. The goal of the democracy voucher system is to "increas[e] transparency, accountability, and accessibility for how Seattle elections are financed."[8] The Supreme Court rejected a challenge to the voucher program in 2019, and it went into effect in 2024.[9]

These public finance systems don't eliminate the influence of Super PACs and outside money in politics. They do, however, level the playing field somewhat.

While *Buckley* and *Citizens United* protect the rights of corporations and Super PACs to pump unlimited sums into political campaigns, candidates who receive public funds may not be nearly as beholden to the special interest organizations, and in turn they may be more free to compromise in service to their constituents. There is still a lack of measurable evidence with which to assess the effect of these reforms. The Brennan Center notes, however, that "if anything, matching fund programs are likely to reduce polarization by encouraging candidates of all kinds to seek new donors, many living in their own districts."[10]

10

The System Exacerbates Division

The institutional protections of incumbency inform my view that government is not equipped to heal our core national divide and reinstitute faith in our institutions. Rather than heal the division between insiders and outsiders that I have identified and examined in this book, the current system actually exacerbates it. The rules that govern campaigns and our political process create cynicism in government and reinforce the view that our institutions are broken.

The protection of incumbency is a major reason our elected officials appear paralyzed, unable to pass legislation or find consensus solutions on a range of issues that concern and frustrate a majority of voters across the political spectrum, like environmental protection, gun violence, and immigration. School shootings persist without policy solutions to make them less common. Our southern border continues to experience a surge in migrants from other countries as we argue over barriers and asylum rules. Carbon emissions escalate without agreements on how to reduce our dependence on fossil fuels and protect our planet.

Rules that reduce incentives to compromise promote absolutist thinking and rhetoric. If incumbents in safe districts can only lose to more extreme primary opponents, their politics become more extreme. Special interest money flows to incumbents, rewarding legislation or obstruction on behalf of the powerful few while diminishing political competition. And our two major political parties have a vested interest in perpetuating this broken system because each benefits from the current rules.

If our leaders continually fail to address the most important issues facing this country and the world, they will become less and less legitimate in the eyes of the people whose interests they are supposed to represent. The fact that the current rules result in both Democrats and Republicans almost never losing reelections leads to widespread cynicism among the electorate. The institutional class of elites is the perceived enemy, rather than one side or the other.

I fear that our current system of government strays a long way from the core principles I learned from Eric Holder, Barack Obama, and Bennie Thompson. Rather than doing the right thing, the men and women we elect to positions of authority too often do the safe thing for their own careers and for their parties. In contrast with Eric Holder's direction to do what's right even if unpopular, legislators retreat to their partisan corners and resist working with, or even being cordial to and respectful of, their political adversaries. In direct contradiction to President Obama's direction to me and other US attorneys to avoid politics in the exercise of our prosecutorial discretion, elected officials prioritize politics over principle and leave important issues that require compromise unaddressed. Rather than "following the facts wherever they lead," as Chairman Thompson directed me to do, our leaders are trying to make facts conform to political narratives. Good government has become a secondary concern to maintaining power, which understandably leads Americans to lose faith in our institutions.

Over the course of the January 6 investigation, I learned that democracy depends on individual decision makers. It relies upon our elected officials' willingness to put the public interest over self-interest, follow the rules, and remain faithful to the immutable principles set forth in our constitution and laws. Vice President Pence did that on January 6 when he refused to accept the slates of fake electors submitted by various states. Georgia secretary of state Brad Raffensperger did that when he resisted President Trump's entreaty to "find 11,780 votes." Officer Caroline Edwards did that when she bravely defended the Capitol as rioters assaulted her and surged toward the building that is home to our representative democracy. These individuals represent the best in government and remind us that good people can and do emerge in crises. We need to do more to encourage others to follow their footsteps, remaining faithful to the rule of law even when it reduces their power or jeopardizes their safety. The future of American democracy depends on our ability to choose the right thing over the easy thing. It is to those solutions that we turn next.

11

"It's Harder to Hate Up Close"

In her bestselling memoir, *Becoming*, Michelle Obama wrote that one of the central lessons she learned about America over the course of her tenure as First Lady was that "it's harder to hate up close." She described meeting people in different regions of the country, from all walks of life. Some were fans, and some were critics. She explained that she often found common ground with others regardless of their political or cultural perspective, or their opinions of her and her husband, simply by spending time with them. "When voters got to see me as a person, they understood that the distorted pictures of me were untrue," she wrote. Mrs. Obama believes that when people take the time to listen to one another, barriers fall and their shared humanity emerges. Her simple but powerful message suggests that basic human connection is the best way to combat hatred, acrimony, and division in America.

Our hatred is palpable these days, and it's stimulated by many of the factors that have been explored in this book — a profit-driven social media apparatus that curates the information we receive and pushes us into echo chambers, governmental authorities who seem to protect the interests of a privileged few, and leaders who exploit and exacerbate the differences among us for political gain. It often seems we are surrounded by voices that reinforce our firmly held convictions. We infrequently interact with or have a chance to learn from people who have opinions or experiences very different from our own, which in turn breeds mistrust and misunderstanding. We tend to fear what we don't understand, and to be judgmental of people different from us. In other words, we hate from a distance, not up close.

Division leads to two fundamental reactions, both of which are destructive in ways that threaten our democracy. Some people get angry at those who are different from them and institutions they perceive to be broken. Their anger manifests in many forms, even violence. Charlottesville and January 6 were spasms of this anger that led to violence fueled, at both events, by people whose rage had reached a boiling point. They were prepared to take extreme measures and risk their safety and liberty in support of strongly held views. They physically assaulted people, causing death and destruction. They also undermined the sense of security of everyone who was present at those events.

Other people have a passive response to the division in our society and their own sense of frustration and distrust — apathy. Rather than get angry and prepare to defend their perspective with violence, they retreat and disengage. These people don't believe it matters if they vote because they feel as if our elected representatives are "all the same." They don't talk or listen to people outside their insular, like-minded circles, as they either are not interested in furthering their understanding or don't want to risk conflict. These people allow their apathy to pull them away from our institutions. They disengage from the processes they believe are broken — government, education, media. They don't get angry, they just stop paying attention.

Anger and apathy are very different reactions to the common problem of cynicism about our institutions, but they share the potential to erode our democracy. Violence is an obvious threat. You can see it play out, as anyone who has watched footage of Charlottesville and January 6 knows. Apathy is more insidious. It cedes power to the people and groups who take action even at times when their opinions and priorities are clearly in the minority. Anger and apathy may have very different immediate effects, but they are both powerful forces eroding the quality of our democracy.

Given their power, they are the central hurdles we must overcome if we are to heal the division that currently afflicts this country. We must recognize, call out, and overcome both our anger and our apathy.

While the challenge presented by the twin threats of anger and apathy is formidable, there is a powerful remedy that has the potential to overcome both forces. As Michelle Obama says, we need to come "up close," pay attention and engage. I'm convinced that if far more people vote, we will have a better, more responsive government. If far more people make an effort to think critically and educate themselves about pressing issues, our democracy will be stronger. If we listen to each other rather than yell at each other, we'll all be smarter. The remedy is us, actively participating and working to protect democracy. Like the police officers who defended the Capitol on January 6, we need to run toward the problem, not away from it. If we can find the will and the methods to do that, we will emerge from this challenging time stronger and more unified than ever.

12

Anger Separates Us

Imagine for a minute a very different sort of Unite the Right rally. What if a group of people motivated by their odious views of racial superiority gathered for a peaceful event. They organized speeches that proudly proclaimed their sense of historic primacy and articulated their shared belief that America has somehow deviated from that tradition. They wore shorts and carried water bottles rather than putting on body armor and carrying shields. They gathered in solidarity to express their collective will rather than to provoke hostility. What if their goal was persuasion rather than confrontation? The anti-racist counter-protesters might still have tried to disrupt this rally, but it would have been a much different event.

Of course, that wasn't the way UTR organizers and attendees approached August 12, 2017, in Charlottesville. Instead, anger was everywhere that day. The event was never intended to be a peaceful protest or a gathering where people made speeches and attempted to recruit followers to their ideology. It was a belligerent mob determined to provoke confrontation. UTR organizers recruited attendees by appealing to their fears, not their hopes. The people who were persuaded by that message came to the event to fight, not to learn or to persuade.

Communications among organizers and attendees that were reviewed as part of the investigation I led demonstrated a determination to provoke opposition and prepare for violence. Eli Mosley was designated UTR's chief of security, and he organized armed groups to escort speakers to and from the event. Many people prepared in advance for violence by gleefully predicting confrontation and expressing a desire to fight, injure, and maim their opponents. They even posted memes about their violent intent in their Discord chats, which were meant to be humorous. One is a photo of John Deere harvesting equipment with the caption "Introducing John Deere's New Multi-Lane Protester Digestor." The poster wrote, "Sure would be nice." The same user suggested putting a "6-8 inch double threaded screw in 2-3 ft axe handles. [If] shit gets real unscrew the bottom and go to town." As the rally drew closer, more and more participants posted photos and selfies of themselves "battle-ready," with their shields, masks, and weapons. At least one selfie featured Trump lawn signs in the background, and in another the poster was wearing a MAKE AMERICA GREAT AGAIN hat.[1]

The crowd that marched in Charlottesville chanted several slogans that reflected their anger and were designed to provoke a violent response. "Jews Will Not Replace Us!" reverberated through the grounds of the University of Virginia on Friday, August 11, and bounced off the walls of buildings in downtown Charlottesville on Saturday, August 12. Those words reflect a warped anti-Semitic frustration with Jewish people and their success. The chant was periodically modified to "You Will Not Replace Us," directed at the diverse gatherings of anti-racist counter-protesters who confronted the rally participants. "Blood and soil," a key slogan of Nazi ideology under Hitler that promoted the vision that only Aryans — members of the so-called master race — should live in Germany or the lands it conquered, similarly echoed through the UTR event. All of these words were chanted at high volume, delivered with vehemence and strong emotion.

The clothes worn by the UTR rally-goers and the items they carried similarly reflected their anger and desire for confrontation: helmets, body armor, flagpoles with sharpened ends, clubs, and shields. They marched in military formation, sending a clear message of preparedness for conflict. The combination of their warlike appearance and their provocative words revealed their true intent — to provoke onlookers to violence, in turn justifying physical confrontation.

The ultimate act of anger that occurred in Charlottesville was the murder of Heather Heyer. James Fields, who had been photographed earlier on August 12 with a shield bearing the insignia of the white nationalist group Vanguard America, drove his Dodge Challenger into a large, diverse crowd of anti-racist counter-protesters. He was later convicted in state court of premeditated murder and pleaded guilty in federal court to a hate crime.[2] While his actions were thankfully unique on August 12, they reflect the extreme antipathy that the UTR participants manifested in Charlottesville.

The hatred expressed by the UTR attendees provoked an angry response, as it was designed to do. The organizers intended conflict all along, though they wanted their violent acts to be cloaked in the faux justification of self-defense. This was made extremely clear in the federal civil lawsuit *Sines v. Kessler*, which held the rally organizers responsible for the violence that occurred in Charlottesville. As Judge Norman K. Moon wrote in his opinion, "Kessler himself told others on Discord to 'bring picket sign post, shields and other self-defense implements which can be turned from a free speech tool to a self-defense weapon should things turn ugly.' And, in the days leading up to the event, he met in person with Defendant Cantwell to plan 'unlawful acts of violence [and] intimidation.'"[3] Rally organizers chose a liberal college town like Charlottesville for this intended show of force, mindful that their event would draw a significant opposition that would likely match their anger and intensity. Those elements created a climate where violence was expected and in their view justified. To some in the crowd that day, the UTR rally was meant to be the first battle in a race war that would continue across the country — a spark to ignite a broader conflict. Outspoken white supremacist Chris Cantwell had even said on a podcast in January 2017, months before the event took place, "Some of us got to be fucking cannon fodder for the race war."[4]

The people who marched to the Capitol on January 6, 2021, were also angry. They had been led to believe that the 2020 presidential election had been stolen from President Trump and that their actions were necessary to prevent an illegitimate election from being certified. Many people at the Capitol believed that they were patriots acting in accord with ancestors who had rebelled against British rule in the American Revolution. They were every bit as angry as those who marched in Charlottesville, though for different reasons.

As in Charlottesville, there was ample discussion of the potential for violence in advance of January 6. As cataloged in great detail in the seditious conspiracy trials that resulted from that day, only to have President Trump pardon the convicted after he was sworn into office on January 20, 2025, many people planned to use violence to interrupt the joint session of Congress. They were determined to prevent the certification of President Biden's election by any means necessary, including pushing through the resistance of police and breaching the building. The Proud Boys and the Oath Keepers prepared for battle, not for a peaceful demonstration. Motivated by their outrage at nonexistent election fraud and the perceived injustice of a stolen election, they were determined to overcome resistance with violence. Oath Keepers' founder Stewart Rhodes felt that "the time for peaceful protest is over" and created an invitation-only Signal group to plan their violent assault, including creating the quick reaction force of firearms stored in Virginia.[5] Many, many other participants also expressed a similar, excited desire to participate in violence. As we summarized in the committee's final report on January 6: "Kenneth Grayson predicted what would eventually happen on January 6th, when on December 23, 2020, he wrote on Facebook that President Trump called people to Washington, DC through his December 19th tweet and then added 'IF TRUMP TELLS US TO STORM THE FUKIN CAPITAL IMA DO THAT THEN!'"[6]

Some demonstrated their intent on January 6 by circulating pre-printed flyers that proclaimed "#OccupyCongress" over images of the United States Capitol. Robert Gieswein, a Coloradan affiliated with the Three Percenters and who was among the first to breach the Capitol, said that he came to Washington, DC, "to keep President Trump in."[7]

President Trump's speech on the Ellipse on the morning of January 6 further inflamed the crowd and stoked its anger. He used violent images, telling the crowd to "fight like hell and if you don't fight like hell, you're not going to have a country anymore."[8] He told his supporters, "We will never give up. We will never concede. It doesn't happen," which suggested to them that there was still a chance that they could prevent the election from being certified. He encouraged those in the crowd to "make [their] voices heard" and told them to march to the Capitol as the joint session was convening. The president's words incited the crowd to do all they could to prevent a perceived injustice. While the president did add "peacefully and patriotically" to his exhortations, the clear intent of his words was to stir the crowd's anger and rally support for a march to the Capitol specifically intended to prevent the certification.

A large number of people were moved by the president's words and took them literally. As Trump's speech wound down in the early afternoon of January 6, those who had been listening to it marched to the Capitol prepared to "fight like hell" to prevent the certification of President Biden's election. They weren't there to make speeches or conduct a free speech rally. To the contrary, many including the organized Proud Boys and Oath Keepers moved to the Capitol determined to use force to achieve their goals.

There could be no more direct manifestation of the anger that characterized the mob at the Capitol on January 6 than the chants of "Hang Mike Pence" that were heard throughout the attack. These angry words were shouted by numerous rioters after the vice president issued a statement declaring his intent to accept the certified slates of electors submitted by the states, as the Constitution required. For following the law, he was vilified as a traitor and threatened with death. Members of the crowd constructed a hangman's noose on the grounds of the Capitol, an ominous warning meant to convey their willingness to use ultimate force to achieve the crowd's goals. Chants of "Where's Nancy" — Speaker of the House Nancy Pelosi — as the mob marched through the Capitol and their possession of zip ties and other items that could be used to restrain were further manifestations of the group's anger at the elected officials who were gathered for the joint session.

As with Charlottesville, it's possible to imagine leaders of the January 6 protest taking a far less confrontational approach. If, for instance, President Trump had made more than an oblique reference to marching "peacefully and patriotically" to the Capitol and instead explicitly discouraged violence, the event could have been a political protest rally rather than a riot. The crowd could have gathered in the shadow of the Capitol at a stage on the National Mall, listened to speeches, and expressed their collective perspective on election integrity, just as other groups have done in that same space for many years. What if the crowd had expressed concern about the election and rallied support for their views rather than unleashing their rage about results that did not go their way and storming the Capitol?

Charlottesville and January 6 were not events designed to win "hearts and minds" or otherwise influence public opinion. They were rather gatherings of angry people, largely white men. They were not "free speech" events, but riots. It is impossible to watch troubling scenes from both well-documented events and not understand the crowd's vehemence and antipathy toward institutions.

Beyond Charlottesville and January 6, there are many other examples of anger surfacing quickly in today's America fueled by similar dynamics: the insider–outsider divide and mistrust of government institutions and democratic processes. The global COVID pandemic, for example, stoked anger at institutions and furthered division in this country. Some people resented government public health mandates and the restrictions on their lives and liberty. They doubted the information they received from authorities and demonized the messengers of the cautious advice provided throughout the pandemic. Division over this topic continues to this very day, with opportunistic politicians and activists engaging in revisionist history based on perceptions, not facts, and using rhetoric intended to incite, not inform. Rather than trusting the experience of Dr. Anthony Fauci and the other professionals tasked with navigating our national response to an unknown new pathogen, many people ascribed sinister motivations to him and other government officials doing their best in the face of an overwhelming challenge. At the same time, people who wanted to place their faith in the experts who held positions of authority resented those who refused to abide by masking, social distancing, and vaccination mandates. They themselves were angry that people were endangering others and taxing our health care system in unreasonable ways.

The national reaction to the pandemic surprised me. At the outset, I thought it could be an opportunity to reinforce our shared humanity and become a unifying force in this country. Much like 9/11, it presented a common enemy that had the potential to highlight how much Americans have in common. That expectation proved to be naive and unrealistic, as the pandemic became yet another wedge used to separate us. It prompted anger rather than sympathy. It resulted in people being suspicious of others' motivations and gave them reasons to resent and demonize rather than coming together in shared suffering and sacrifice. Something that had potential to unify ended up stoking division — a sad reminder of the polarized times in which we live.

There are numerous examples of significant events and issues that demonstrate and reinforce anger at our institutions. *New York Times* columnist Frank Bruni wrote a book on this subject called *The Age of Grievance* in which he details the many manifestations of American anger, and the fact that it comes from both sides of the political spectrum.[9] He points out that while grievance has fueled social change throughout American history, it seems these days to be particularly personal. "Not all grievances are created equal," he writes. "There is January 6, 2021, and there is everything else. Attempts by leaders on the right to minimize what happened that day and lump it together with protests on the left are as ludicrous as they are dangerous . . . But it's also true that on both sides of the political divide, there's a quickness to grievance, a tendency among many people to identify themselves and interpret events in terms of past, current, and looming hurts . . . It's not so much bipartisan as it is pan-partisan or supra-partisan, and it's getting worse."

13

Anger as Motivation for Change

I don't mean to suggest that skepticism about institutions is a bad thing. American history is full of examples of people whose criticism of institutions ultimately improved them and made this country more equitable and just. From the American Revolution to the Civil Rights Movement, intentional violations of law have exposed injustice and motivated important steps toward freedom and equality. My point here isn't to criticize strong opposition or even rejection of systems. Rather it is to point out that our core divisions center on the question of whether American institutions should be respected and regarded as vehicles that can serve the common good and as a means to settle our differences civilly — even when reforms are needed or when the political opposition happens to be in the majority — or whether they should be feared, rejected, even destroyed.

As Frank Bruni notes, American resistance to injustice has motivated many important changes in law and life throughout our history. Anger at institutions has inspired cultural and political change and led to reforms almost universally embraced in retrospect. Dissent is fundamentally American and must be recognized as an engine for reform. The bedrock of democracy is the citizen's ability to criticize authority, a core freedom that has separated America from other nations and shaped our national character and policy for generations.

There is, however, a fundamental difference between the productive dissent that motivated the Civil Rights Movement and today's palpable anger at institutions. What we are experiencing today is reflexive anger, not necessarily one motivated by a specific goal or cause. It is reactive, not proactive. For instance, people with disparate motivations came together in Charlottesville and in the attack on the Capitol in a common cause against a system they believe fails to protect their interests and rights. Resistance to institutions that they believed no longer protected their privilege was the cause around which they rallied, not some broader legal, social, or policy objective. Their goal was anti-democratic, as it sought to protect some, not all, which is the antithesis of the civil-rights-era idea that the expansion of rights and justice for one group does not diminish the rights of others.

While Anger at institutions can motivate change, it

can also become self-fulfilling and self-perpetuating. Anger breeds more anger. Cynicism in government discourages participation and undercuts the ability of institutions that depend on democratic participation and compromise to be effective. Anger can separate us and make democracy less productive, which in turn furthers anger and fuels increased skepticism. Many people are trapped in this cycle today and find numerous examples of dysfunctional institutions that reinforce their anger.

14

Apathy and Alienation

Not everyone who believes our institutions are broken is outraged. Those who are more apathetic than angry withdraw rather than engage. To these cynics, the system is irretrievably broken. They don't believe their personal participation matters, as the problems are too large and intractable for them to make a difference.

There are lots of examples of the ways apathy can be more damaging to our democratic system than eruptions of anger or even political violence. A surprisingly low number of people in this country actually exercise their right to vote. In the 2020 presidential election, about two-thirds of eligible voters actually cast a ballot.[1] A total of approximately 154 million people voted in that election.[2] That means about 77 million Americans who were eligible to vote failed to participate — a shockingly high number. Of those 77 million, about 12.8 million were registered to vote yet did not. The US Census Bureau conducted a survey of eligible voters who did not participate. The results show that "not being interested in the election" was the primary reason people did not vote, followed closely by dislike of candidates and campaign issues, and being too busy or having a conflicting schedule.[3]

When so many Americans choose not to register to vote or cast a ballot, it gives those who do participate disproportionate clout. More specifically, their votes are worth one-third more than they would otherwise be. The enhanced value of each vote gives outsized power to more extreme perspectives and policy positions. People whose vote is motivated, for example, by a desire to support a progressive cause like the Green New Deal may represent 15 percent of the vote in a particular election. We don't know whether the one-third of voters who did not participate support the Green New Deal in the same proportion. Similarly, 25 percent of the voters in a state election may be motivated by the desire to outlaw abortion in that jurisdiction. That percentage of voters doesn't mean that a quarter of the people in that state support a complete abortion ban, as the large number of non-participants may have a different view. In short, lack of participation cedes political power to people with special interests.

Apathy also makes people less motivated to stay informed about issues that directly affect their own lives and the well-being of others. In August 2022, only

38 percent of Americans indicated that they follow the news "all or most of the time," according to a Pew Research Center survey.[4] Another 19 percent follow the news "only now and then," and 9 percent said they "hardly ever" follow the news. These figures are down about 15 percent since 2016, when 51 percent of Americans indicated that they followed the news "all or most of the time" and only 5 percent said they "hardly ever" consumed news.[5] Distrust of the news media is particularly acute among Republicans. In 2022, 37 percent of self-identified Republicans followed the news "all or most of the time," a 20 percent drop from 2016 when 57 percent of Republicans indicated that level of interest in news. Among Democrats, the percentage that follows the news "all or most of the time" dropped 7 percent between 2016 and 2022.

The Pew findings demonstrate that declining interest in news is fueled largely by distrust of the media among a wide array of Americans. Gallup has been polling Americans regarding their "trust and confidence in the news media" every year since 1974. In 2022, 38 percent of Americans responded "none at all" to the question of whether they had such trust and confidence. This percentage is up sharply in the past four years and up substantially since the 1970s.[6]

The distrust in media reflected by the Gallup findings skews younger and Republican, as those groups tend to be more skeptical about the veracity of television, radio, and newspaper reporting.

Americans are not only withdrawing from news and politics but also are participating in other forms of civic and community life to a much lesser degree than in previous years. Church attendance in the United States, for example, declined more than 10 percent between 2000 and 2023. According to a recent Gallup survey, only three in ten Americans regularly attend a religious service of any kind.[7] This decline is evident across denominations and regions of the country and, as with a lack of interest in news coverage, is particularly marked among younger adults. Union membership has declined by 50 percent in the past thirty years,[8] as has membership in professional and civic organizations.

A recent poll conducted by the *Wall Street Journal* and the University of Chicago found declining rates of belief in institutions that have motivated Americans for years. For example, only 38 percent of survey respondents indicated that "patriotism" is very important to them, down from 70 percent in 1998.[9] Only 39 percent said religious faith is very important to them, down from 62 percent over that same span. Only 27 percent of survey respondents indicated that community involvement is very important to them, down from about 50 percent in 1982. These responses reflect the core reality of cynicism among Americans and reflect our lack of community connection and increasing polarization.

Widespread withdrawal from endeavors that enhance community leads to increasing isolation among Americans. The bipartisan Joint Economic Committee of the United States House of Representatives published a report in 2019 that revealed the percentage of Americans who reported talking with neighbors at least a couple of times per month declined from 71 percent to just more than 50 percent between 2008 and 2018.[10] According to a 2023 Pew study, "A narrow majority of adults (53 percent) say they have between one and four close friends, while . . . some 8 percent say they have no close friends," and younger generations report having fewer friends than older generations.[11] As independent journalist Anne Helen Petersen writes on this topic, her specialty, "My theory is that retirees have more time, sure, but they're also just generally more practiced at the infrastructure of community and friendship. They're not the peak 'joiners' that their parents were in the post-war period, but they grew up in households that were much more likely to have strong connections to religious and community organizations in some capacity."[12] In other words, the new norm for Americans is loneliness.

Some of the isolation we are experiencing is a reflection of our access to and use of technology. People can shop, obtain entertainment, and communicate without directly interacting with other people in real time. Our ability to access basic services via technology decreases time spent in communal settings. Even before the rise of the internet and smartphones, the loss of "third spaces" — a term first coined by sociologist Ray Oldenburg in 1989 — was being widely studied and discussed as a growing, and concerning, phenomenon.[13] A third space is one that is not home (the first space) or work (the second place), but rather a third place where people socialize and build community: churches, bowling alleys, Elk lodges or American Legion halls — anyplace people regularly gather to interact with others in person can fit the bill. The problem has become greatly exacerbated since it was first identified and studied in 1989. Back then, the biggest challenges to third spaces were American zoning laws and automobile culture. Folks would go home and stay at home rather than go around the corner, down the street, or across the neighborhood to a gathering place. Technology changed people's habits for the worse, and in a post-pandemic world, fewer of these spaces even exist. Instead of finding ways outside of work and home to connect with others, many Americans withdraw into social media platforms and other electronic means of engagement.

These declines in participation reflect widespread alienation in America, not just from one another but also from the government that is supposed to serve, and reflect, us all. The University of Chicago study indicates that almost half of Americans (49 percent) feel "more and more like a stranger in my own country."[14] According to a study from nonpartisan research organization Public Agenda, nearly one in three adults feels "politically alienated": 34 percent of Republicans, 29 percent of independents, and 25 percent of Democrats.[15] Fully half of all Americans believe that "democracy is in crisis," a figure that has sharply increased over the past several years. "Politicians don't represent me. They are only responsible for corporations and large funders," one twenty-nine-year-old female Democrat respondent from South Dakota told researchers. "I don't believe any politician on either side. Everybody votes on party lines and with so much polarization, nothing ever gets done. Politicians are solely focused on their own interests," said a twenty-three-year-old female Republican from Oklahoma. The study found that 66 percent of Americans consider it a serious problem that politicians are more interested in blocking the other party than in getting anything done.[16]

This widespread feeling of alienation also has dangerous potential in terms of actual violence. The most startling of the University of Chicago study's findings was that 28 percent of voters believe that "it may become necessary at some point to take up arms against the government."[17] This view is held by one in three Republicans and one in five Democrats — a surprisingly high number of people across the political spectrum who are so disengaged that they are inclined to justify the use of force against the government. This finding shows that apathy and anger may actually be related in a continuum of cynicism about institutions. Apathy leads to alienation, which leads to desperation and potential violence. We risk slipping into a dangerous pattern of self-perpetuating dysfunction. The more we get angry or apathetic, the less functional our system becomes, which in turn reinforces cynicism about democracy and the value of participating in its processes or safeguarding its institutions.

15

Maintaining Community

According to Pew Research, 65 percent of Americans always or often feel "exhausted" when they think about politics.[1] This discouraging finding represents yet another step on the slippery slope toward national apathy. I can empathize. It's difficult to put forth effort when you know that many others aren't paying attention and those that are will strongly disagree with you in disagreeable ways. I have wondered whether any of the work I've done on the Charlottesville and January 6 investigations actually educated and informed people in ways that influenced their opinions. I hope the verified facts our work revealed have mattered, though I fear that in both instances we were largely preaching to the choir, speaking to people who were outraged by these horrific events and were more interested in having ammunition to support their opinions than in gaining understanding and growing.

I resist that feeling of exhaustion and continue to believe that the serious problems we face are neither permanent nor intractable. Despite having spent so much time immersed in the awful facts surrounding the Unite the Right rally and the January 6 attack on the Capitol, I remain hopeful about the future of our democracy. Even after spending years as a federal prosecutor focused on heinous crimes and brutal acts of violence, I believe people are essentially good and will choose to do the right thing the vast majority of the time. I have faith in our collective resilience, ability to learn from history, and fundamental humanity. That faith outweighs my concern about the ugliness and division that my work has revealed.

What informs my faith in our potential is the belief that the remedy to these problems is actually quite simple. We need to find ways to establish and maintain community and enhance the connection to one another. We have to appreciate that we are much more alike than we are different. By and large, we want the same things for our families and for our country, even if we disagree in a multitude of ways about the best ways to achieve them and about the role of government. We should emphasize the ways in which we are alike — our common aspirations, values, and priorities. Our nation is unique in its rich diversity of perspective, culture, and experience. We should celebrate that diversity and use it to enhance our understanding of the challenges we face.

I appreciate that the "simple" solution described above sounds both vague and unrealistic. How exactly can we come together, enhance community, and celebrate our diverse perspectives? Is that even possible given the statistics about levels of anger and apathy in our nation, and the polarization that we have all come to expect? How we respond to and learn from Charlottesville and January 6 and the common threats to our democracy that persist today will determine the future of our country, and of each of us and those we love. Looking back at those two events, we first need to recognize and reinforce the positive forces that prevented worse outcomes, and then we need to hold accountable those whose actions threatened public safety. Looking forward, we need to use the lessons of Charlottesville and January 6 as motivation to promote community. Seen with clarity, Charlottesville and January 6 can light the path toward a better future — one we should all aspire to follow.

16

Courage and Accountability

Throughout my years as a federal prosecutor, I witnessed both heart-wrenching tragedy and inspirational courage. I spent years immersed in the worst moments of people's lives. I asked robbery victims to recount the incidents in which their property was stolen, sexual assault victims to describe the abuse they suffered, and fraud victims to tell me how they were misled. I saw a range of emotions in these meetings — shame, sorrow, anger, and vengeance. Almost no one who came to my office was happy to be there. The people with whom I dealt were either profoundly affected by a loss they could not undo or reluctant to assist in holding others accountable.

In the midst of this tableau of tragedy, I also witnessed heroism, courage, forgiveness, and mercy. Witnesses came forward to describe the violence they observed, despite the very real risks their cooperation created for themselves and their families. I saw dogged detectives pursue every lead with determination to hold those responsible accountable. I saw overworked defense lawyers zealously defend their clients despite caseloads that far exceeded mine. I appeared before judges who carefully considered my arguments, tried to make just decisions, and endeavored to impose fair sentences. Out of the darkness in the cases that fill the dockets of criminal courts around the country, people find light, integrity, and purpose. Tragedy creates opportunities for heroism.

Perhaps no one embodies this reality more than Carol Watkins, the mother of a homicide victim in a case I handled as an assistant US attorney in Washington, DC. Carol's son Anthony Watkins was one of more than a dozen men murdered by a violent drug gang that I prosecuted in the early 2000s. Our star witness in the trial of the gang members responsible for these killings was a man named Oscar Veal, who functioned as a paid assassin for the gang and killed seven people. Veal pleaded guilty to all seven murders, including Anthony Watkins's, and agreed to describe each one for the jury, including the direction and compensation he received from the gang leaders. Ms. Watkins sat in court and listened as Veal described how and why he murdered her son.

At every criminal sentencing in federal court, victims have the right to present information to the sentencing judge about ways in which the crimes at issue have affected them. When Carol Watkins addressed the court at Veal's sentencing, I was braced for condemnation and expected her to ask the judge to sentence the man who killed her son to a lengthy prison term. Ms. Watkins turned and faced Mr. Veal — choosing to direct her remarks to him rather than the judge. In a hushed courtroom, she told Mr. Veal, "I love you. I pray for you. And I forgive you." Everyone was stunned. In a thoughtful, measured voice, she explained that her Christian faith prevents her from judging others, seeking vengeance, or passing judgment on people for the worst things they've done. To the contrary, she explained, her faith compels her to love and forgive those whose transgressions have harmed her. She told Mr. Veal and everyone in that hushed courtroom that she had to choose love over hate, as doing so was the only way she could continue to live in a world without her son.

I recall weeping as Ms. Watkins spoke that day, incredibly moved by her grace and compassion. Her act of forgiveness toward a man who had taken her son from her left an indelible mark on me. It represented the very highest form of human dignity, well beyond what I thought possible or could have summoned myself in that moment. She demonstrated that tragedy creates an opportunity to assert values. She showed me that trying times test our resolve, our perspective, and our ability to move ahead. Carol Watkins turned her loss into a test of her faith, her values, and her approach to life. I have aspired to follow her example in response to the tragedies in my own life.

The story of Carol Watkins is relevant to Charlottesville and January 6, because in studying those two tragedies, I found heroism, courage, strength, and fidelity to purpose. Any account of those horrific events must include an acknowledgment that there were numerous people who, like Carol Watkins, responded to darkness with light. These heroes countered the threats posed by the white supremacists in Charlottesville and the angry mob at the Capitol by adherence to core values — duty, bravery, and the rule of law. But for their heroic actions, the outcomes could have been far worse. Their actions also help us understand the way forward and reinforce what should be a personal commitment to preserving and protecting democracy.

It is also important to acknowledge the legal responses to the events in Charlottesville and at the Capitol, which sought to impose accountability. The news media widely covered thorough efforts by law enforcement officers at all levels of government to bring those who engaged in political violence to justice, although President Trump's pardoning of all Capitol Hill rioters, even those accused of or already found guilty of the most serious offenses, halted all ongoing investigations and prosecutions. Lesser known, however, are the efforts of civil plaintiffs to use the courts to provide accountability, raise awareness, and limit the potential for future lawlessness. One group has invoked a Virginia statute that prevents unofficial militia activity in a suit designed to prevent the white supremacy organizations that marched on Charlottesville from returning. Other plaintiffs have invoked federal civil rights statutes to hold the rally organizers accountable for the damage they caused. Similarly, civil cases have followed the attack on the Capitol. Capitol Police officers and other plaintiffs sued Donald Trump for his role in inciting insurrection after losing reelection in 2020. These cases represent slow-moving but potentially significant steps toward holding people responsible for their actions.

While the heroism shown in Charlottesville and Washington and the steps toward accountability are significant, they do not address the systemic issues and conditions that allowed these threats to our democracy to coalesce in the first place, and are still ongoing. While good people prevented worse outcomes in these two crucial instances, their actions do not resolve the broader systemic issues that motivated each event. Accountability will not heal the underlying division in our society that these events revealed. America needs forward-looking solutions that are sweeping in nature. While law enforcement, advocacy groups, and victims of political violence should be lauded for their efforts to hold those for January 6 and Charlottesville accountable, it's up to we the people, of all political stripes, to address dynamics that pose the greatest threats to democracy and create the conditions for political violence.

17

Democracy Comes Down to Us

Many brave men and women demonstrated individual responsibility and emerged as heroes in the midst of the searing tragedies of 2017 and 2021. The events in Charlottesville started with a local debate about the presence of Civil War statues in two downtown parks. A high school student, Zyahna Bryant, started the discussion by submitting a petition to the city council asking that the statue of Robert E. Lee be removed. In announcing the petition, Bryant wrote, "When I think of Robert E. Lee, I instantly think of someone fighting in favor of slavery. Thoughts of physical harm, cruelty, and disenfranchisement flood my mind."[1] Bryant was soon joined by a chorus of other local activists who similarly objected to the statue. Their efforts led to the creation of the Blue Ribbon Commission on Race, Memorials and Public Spaces, which gathered community input and considered the future of the statues. This group of local activists generated an important public discussion about not only the Civil War statues but also race, history, shared public spaces, and ultimately our values as a community.

As the UTR event came into focus, many people in Charlottesville prepared to counter the hateful speech they knew was coming their way. The Reverend Seth Wispelwey was one of those people. Reverend Wispelwey is an ordained minister of the United Church of Christ and an organizer of an interfaith group called Congregate C'ville, which brought together Jewish, Catholic, Protestant, and Muslim groups aligned in their common desire to counter the UTR participants. Reverend Wispelwey and Congregate C'ville organized nonviolent resistance training for antiracist activists to prepare them to confront the permitted event with civil disobedience, risking arrest and assault. On August 12, 2017, the reverend was part of a diverse group of people who locked arms and attempted to block access to the park where the rally was to be held. He was pushed aside and assaulted. "If white supremacy is the governing and prevailing order, and white supremacists threaten violence and do violence and are looking for violence, you can't ignore it because it is the oxygen we breathe," he told journalist Nora Neus in her oral history book *24 Hours in Charlottesville* about why he decided to take action.[2]

Lieutenant Joseph Hatter of the Charlottesville Police Department (CPD) was positioned just steps away from Reverend Wispelwey's attempted blockade of the park. Lieutenant Hatter was a zone commander, assigned to lead a group of officers stationed immediately across the street from the park where the permitted rally was to take place. On the morning of August 12, Lieutenant Hatter waded into the crowd to de-escalate conflicts between attendees. In one incident, "Lieutenant Hatter jumped over the barricade to de-escalate the tension between [a] flag-toting demonstrator and the crowd around him . . . Hatter spoke a few words to calm the demonstrator down," our report found. "This is the only instance we identified of a CPD officer leaving a barricaded safe zone to enter the crowd and de-escalate a potentially violent situation on August 12."[3] Rather than follow his supervisors' directive that he stay behind the barricades, Lieutenant Hatter attempted to prevent violence before it occurred. Upon declaration of the unlawful assembly, Lieutenant Hatter was called to lead his officers away from their assigned zone to don riot gear and prepare to disperse the crowd. During our independent review of these events, Lieutenant Hatter expressed his frustration: "We were prevented from doing police work," he told me. "People [were] getting hurt, and I'm standing around behind a steel fence."[4]

His actions stand in stark contrast with the other CPD and Virginia State Police (VSP) officers who stood by while violence unfolded.

After the unlawful assembly was declared and the park cleared, Heather Heyer was part of a group of anti-racist protesters who moved through Charlottesville looking to prevent confrontations between the alt-right attendees and local residents. She was in a large crowd at the intersection of Fourth and Water Streets when white nationalist James Fields drove his Dodge Charger into them. Heyer was killed, and many others were seriously injured. Heather Heyer sacrificed her life protesting against hate. There can be no greater example of fidelity to purpose and putting yourself at risk for your beliefs. "If you're not outraged, you're not paying attention," Heather posted on Facebook shortly before she died.[5]

Heyer's mother, Susan Bro, is another hero to come out of the events of the summer of 2017. She has picked up Heather's mantle of advocating for racial justice, establishing a foundation in Heather's name and speaking out against injustices in Charlottesville and beyond. "Before this, I was a government employee, so I kind of kept my opinions to myself, a little bit," she told the *Washington Post* with a laugh. "Heather and I were definitely on the same page a lot politically, and when we weren't, we would talk it out. Now people want my opinion, so fine, I have things to say. It's not that I never had them before. I've always had things to say, just nobody was willing to listen, and now people are asking me, and so I'm speaking." Ms. Bro has said that she wants to make her daughter Heather's death "count."[6]

In the aftermath of the UTR event, city manager Maurice Jones faced a dilemma. Criticism of CPD, the city council, and other parts of city government immediately followed the rally. Lawyers and insurers advised Mr. Jones to refrain from making any admissions or taking steps that could support litigation against the city. He ignored that advice and commissioned an independent review of the events of the "summer of hate" in Charlottesville. "As our City continues to recover from the rallies that brought great hate into our community, we must take time to reflect on our operational response to these tragic events," he said in his announcement.[7] Mindful of the risk that a review would reveal facts exposing the ineffectiveness or negligence of city officials, Mr. Jones believed that an independent review of the facts and circumstances of the UTR and other events was essential to healing and restoring public confidence in government. In announcing the review, he pledged that it would be fully independent and proceed with full access to city personnel and information. He further promised to disclose the results of the review to the public upon its completion. His willingness to launch a review and examine the city's failures was an example of effective leadership, and it led to the credible accounting of events that I have relied on for this book.

There are multiple examples I could cite of heroes whose actions on and around January 6 helped preserve democracy. Like Lieutenant Hatter, there were many brave men and women in law enforcement who risked their lives to protect others in the Capitol building. US Capitol Police officer Caroline Edwards continued to protect the west front of the Capitol after receiving a concussion when rioters pushed past her at the Peace Circle. She bravely described her experience to a national audience at the first prime-time hearing of the January 6 committee.[8] Metropolitan Police Department officer Michael Fanone was pulled into the crowd and viciously beaten by rioters, escaping only when he referenced his young daughter and pleaded for his life. Officers Daniel Hodges, Aquilino Gonell, and Harry Dunn joined Officer Fanone in describing their experience protecting the Capitol on January 6 in the select committee's first hearing in the summer of 2021.[9] There were hundreds of men and women who similarly repelled violence that day. But for their bravery and courage in the face of great danger, the insurrection may have been successful.

In the days before January 6, numerous state officials performed their duties with honor and fidelity to the rule of law, even in the face of extreme pressure from President Trump and his co-conspirators. Election workers like Ruby Freeman and her daughter Shaye Moss counted ballots in Georgia with diligence and fairness. President Trump falsely accused them of fraud in multiple tweets, which resulted in threats to their lives.[10] As a federal judge later found, they were defamed by President Trump's lawyer Rudy Giuliani, who similarly accused them of surreptitiously miscounting votes.[11] In Pennsylvania, Al Schmidt was Philadelphia city commissioner and the lone Republican on a three-member municipal board tasked with overseeing the conduct of elections in that city. In a November 11, 2020, tweet, President Trump accused Schmidt of "refus[ing] to look into a mountain of dishonesty and corruption" in the counting of votes in Philadelphia.[12] Like Freeman and Moss, Schmidt was subject to vile death threats by Trump supporters.

While Freeman, Moss, and Schmidt have received the most attention, false accusations of voter fraud led to similar threats to election workers around the country. Dozens of poll workers and ballot counters were vilified and threatened due to unfounded allegations.

Our elections in this country are facilitated by thousands of public servants, both paid and volunteer, who work diligently to conduct fair vote counts. You see some of them when you vote — the men and women sitting at tables, checking identification and providing ballots. Others are unseen — working in nondescript government buildings to keep track of voter registration, establish and maintain polling stations, facilitate absentee and mail-in voting, and broadly ensure that every eligible voter can cast his or her ballot in an impartial, nonpartisan process. The men and women who run our elections do so with honor and integrity, performing their important responsibilities largely in anonymity. Their careful adherence to law ensures that our elections are conducted fairly and impartially. The fact that some of them have been vilified due to the unfair criticism of the voting process makes their service even more heroic, as it puts them at risk.

Elected officials similarly stepped up to defend democracy in the days after the 2020 election. Georgia secretary of state Brad Raffensperger supervised the conduct of the 2020 election in his state. His office investigated numerous allegations of voter fraud and conducted three complete audits of the results, all of which confirmed that President Biden won the presidential election in Georgia. He explained all of this to President Trump in a telephone call on January 3, just three days before the attack on the Capitol. Secretary Raffensperger stood firm in the face of direct pressure to "find 11,780 votes." Like the poll workers described above, his rejection of false theories of fraud subjected Secretary Raffensperger and his family to vile threats. Arizona Speaker of the House Rusty Bowers, another Republican, similarly rejected President Trump's direct encouragement to take official action based on nonexistent voter fraud. Like Secretary Raffensperger, Speaker Bowers said no. These brave state officials stayed true to their duty to the Constitution, despite overwhelming public pressure from the president of the United States.

There were voices inside the White House who similarly tried to ensure a peaceful transition of power after the 2020 election. Foremost among those was White House counsel Pat Cipollone, who helped prevent his client, the president of the United States, from taking extreme action to pursue baseless allegations of voter fraud. Cipollone was one of several White House advisers who instructed the president that there was no basis to seize voting machines or appoint a special counsel to investigate voter fraud during a meeting on the evening of December 18.[13] He also strongly opposed the president's appointment of Jeffrey Clark as acting attorney general, telling the president in an Oval Office meeting on January 3 that doing so would not change the core reality of an absence of evidence of voter fraud and would result in mass resignations at the Department of Justice. On January 6, Cipollone opposed the president's proposed trip to the Capitol during the joint session and repeatedly encouraged him to issue a stronger statement directing his followers to leave the Capitol. "I felt it was my obligation to continue to push for that, and others felt it was their obligation as well," he told the select committee. "My view was that we should do as much as we possibly can as quickly as possible." In that same interview before the select committee, Cipollone explained that he seriously thought about resigning his position as White House counsel between the election and the inauguration of President Biden but was concerned about who might replace him.[14] He did not resign, and as a result, he remained a calm voice of reason in opposition to others pursuing an unlawful strategy to maintain power.

Vice President Pence is another hero of January 6. He repeatedly told the president that he did not have the legal authority to reject certified slates of electors submitted by the official authorities in each state. Nonetheless, the president privately berated him as weak, and publicly claimed that the vice president did have authority to unilaterally reject these certified slates of electors. Despite that pressure, the vice president remained faithful to his constitutional duty on January 6. His refusal to bow to that pressure led President Trump to issue a tweet during the attack on the Capitol alleging that he lacked courage, resulting in the crowd furiously chanting, “Hang Mike Pence.” After coming within forty feet of the angry mob during his evacuation from the Senate chamber,[15] the vice president calmly worked (from a loading dock beneath the Capitol) with military and law enforcement leaders to ensure the resources necessary to disperse the crowd and resume the joint session. His actions on January 6 reflect a fidelity to duty and the rule of law above and beyond his personal safety and political self-interest.

Many of the heroes who helped preserve democracy on January 6 were lifelong Republicans, members of President Trump's own party, who put the Constitution over their political self-interest, and their country over their party. They recognized that maintenance of democracy depends upon adherence to certain immutable principles, like the people's right to choose their leaders. They stayed faithful to that core value on January 6, which prevented the anti-democratic outcome of a successful insurrection.

People often ask me what surprised me most about the two seminal events I was tasked with investigating. I frequently respond by saying that I was most surprised by how close the attack on the Capitol and all of the attendant factors that led to that event came to succeeding in preventing the transfer of power. The fact that it didn't work shows me that democracy is earned, not given. The individual stories of courage outlined above show that democracy comes down to individual decision makers and their willingness to adhere to the bedrock principles on which this country was founded. Democracy comes down to us. Everyone who enjoys the freedom that comes with living in a democratic society has the responsibility to protect and defend the values that ensure that freedom. Thankfully, people responded to that challenge in Charlottesville and at the Capitol on January 6. Whether we will respond to future challenges with similar strength and courage depends on no one other than us.

18

Balloons

One of the primary responsibilities of a United States attorney is relationship building. During my five years serving as US attorney for the Western District of Virginia, I spent a lot of time driving around Virginia, cultivating and maintaining relationships with a range of stakeholders who came into contact with the work of our office. I met with police chiefs, sheriffs, and other state and local law enforcement personnel. I met with elected officials, business leaders, and representatives of nonprofit and charitable organizations. My intention was to bring a holistic approach to public safety — a union of targeted enforcement, crime prevention, and reentry support for people released from prison. I analogized this vision of public safety to a three-legged stool and became an evangelist for the necessity of providing support for prevention and reentry programs in the communities in which we were targeting our enforcement efforts. I even carried a stool around in the trunk of my car to use as an illustration in sketching out this approach during these meetings.

One of the most poignant days I had during my time as US attorney was a visit to the campus of Virginia Tech in Blacksburg on April 16, 2010. It was the third anniversary of a campus mass shooting that took the lives of thirty-one people. I went to Tech to meet with the law enforcement leaders who responded to that awful tragedy as well as to attend various memorial services. I spent a lot of time with the federal agents from the Bureau of Alcohol, Tobacco and Firearms who had been among the first on the scene, and I heard them describe both the violence they witnessed and the emotional toll the incident had taken on them since.

That cool April morning started for me on the Virginia Tech drill field — a large grassy lawn in the center of campus in front of the building where the shooting took place. When I arrived at the drill field, I was part of a large crowd of hundreds, even thousands, of people who were gathered to participate in the "Run in Remembrance," a 3.1-mile run through the campus dedicated to the memories of the thirty-one victims. Each of us was given a balloon, either maroon or orange, the Virginia Tech school colors. We were instructed to move toward the starting line for what would be a silent start to the run. A cluster of thirty-one white balloons floated up over the quiet crowd of strangers. As the white balloons ascended skyward, runners in the crowd started releasing the maroon and orange balloons we'd been given. There was no direction to do so, but as more and more balloons rose, everyone released theirs. What ensued was absolutely beautiful — a sea of maroon and orange balloons, rising up toward the thirty-one white balloons that had gone first.

I have told that story many times since 2010, as I think the symbol of the balloons rising over the drill field is the perfect illustration of how communities can come together in the wake of tragedy. The silent communication of the symbolic release was so meaningful, as it showed that a large group of strangers connected to one another through a common sense of purpose were linked by their shared humanity, their grief, and their desire to help one another recover from that awful tragedy. What united us was far more powerful and important than any differences — religious, socioeconomic, political — that might separate us in our daily lives.

The balloon story presents a good analogy about what I believe is ultimately necessary to heal the division in America and preserve democracy. In response to the violence in Charlottesville and at the Capitol, we need to come together and connect rather than retreat to the warring tribes that so often define us. We need to focus on what we have in common, as those commonalities are far more significant than our differences. Ironically, one thing a majority of Americans share is a sense of frustration with the polarization gripping our politics and culture. We need to find ways to listen to, learn from, and respect one another, then ultimately recommit to some common values. We can't rely on elected officials, individual heroes, the court system, or any other outside source to mend what's broken in America. A variety of dynamics in our political system have led us to a point where American democracy itself is at risk. We've lost sight of the fact that our democracy works only when people have faith in the institutions upon which we rely to settle our differences. The balance has tipped away from a system that works for the people, and the only way to correct the situation is for us to do it ourselves, to find ways to promote community over division.

Admittedly, coming together is easier said than done. I've explored in great detail in this book many forces at play in America that push us apart. An information landscape fueled by social media algorithms and for-profit news models keeps us in silos and reinforces our prevailing beliefs. We live in gerrymandered districts that see little political competition and almost no compromise. Primaries that are controlled by the two major political parties and fueled by special interest money reward extreme rhetoric and an unwillingness to compromise. So many of us are angry, or apathetic, or both. Any effort to heal our division will have to overcome these forces. Unity is upstream, so we'll have to struggle to achieve it.

Despite these odds and the forces arrayed against us, I believe America can come together and heal its current division. Doing so will require engagement, participation, and willingness to take personal responsibility for the maintenance of democracy. It will take a concerted, grassroots effort that inspires, motivates, and appeals to our hopes and aspirations. It will take attention and effort, rather than complacency. Healing will take sustained attention to what unites us, and a willingness to listen, compromise, and admit mistakes.

To fix our broken democracy, we should pursue three basic goals. First, we should do all we can to encourage people to participate and make it easy for them to vote, stay informed, and voice their concerns. Second, we need to find ways to teach and model constructive engagement, giving people the tools to sift information, pursue and consider alternative points of view, and listen to and learn from their fellow citizens. This should start early in public schools that help young people navigate the systems by which they receive information and encourage them to pursue the first goal of participation. Finally, we need to create systems for Americans to come together in common purpose — working together in service to their communities and finding ways to help one another. If we commit to pursue these three foundational goals, America will heal itself.

People across the political divide believe in the importance of contributing to the greater good, the benefits of pursuing knowledge, and the idea that community makes us stronger. The irony of the division I've seen in my work in Charlottesville and in Congress is that it is inconsistent with the fact that Americans share so many fundamental priorities. We have more in common than we do differences. Our shared values and goals make me optimistic about our nation's ability to come together around core principles of democracy — in other words, how we reach compromise solutions without political violence. While the events of recent years reveal the existence of strong disagreements, they do not alter the fact that all of us want to live in freedom to pursue happiness, create productive lives for our families, and live in a world that is fundamentally just and humane.

19

Facilitating Participation in Public Life

The very essence of democracy is self-governance. The founding fathers understood that a government of, by, and for the people would have more legitimacy than a monarchy, as everyone governed has an opportunity to shape the rules by which they live. To maintain their status, elected officials must be responsive to those they represent, or not get reelected. In a real sense, they are representatives, tasked with giving voice to the priorities and perspectives of their constituents.

While this process makes sense in theory, it doesn't often work in practice. American democracy has been on a path for many years to increased polarization. The success of the democratic process working in ways that promote the common good depends on the willingness of people to hold their representatives accountable. Citizens must voice their concerns to their elected leaders and ensure that those views are reflected in the actions of those leaders. In my view, participation is a fundamental obligation of anyone who lives in a democracy. When people fail to voice concerns and do not vote, they cede their democratic authority to those who do. Our government becomes less representative and more prone to pursue the objectives of subsets of individuals who more consistently make their voices heard and are more susceptible to manipulation by a range of interest groups, misinformation, toxic algorithms, and other dynamics that threaten democracy. Low levels of participation in the political process makes our system less democratic, as it represents the interests and opinions of far fewer citizens than it should.

The first and most basic responsibility of citizenship is voting. Casting one's ballot for leaders who manage our public schools, levy taxes, consider policy responses to emerging challenges, and navigate our country's place in world affairs is the obligation of every American. Failing to do so makes our government less responsive to the needs of the majority and cedes power to voices who protect special interests. Full participation, starting with voting, is the only way to ensure that government acts in the interests of all citizens.

To facilitate this core requirement of full participation, we must make it easier to vote. We have traditionally held elections on Tuesdays in November primarily during business hours. While this method works for most Americans, on any given Election Day a considerable percentage of eligible voters cannot physically travel to a polling station due to professional or family obligations, infirmity or illness, lack of transportation, or other factors. To accommodate those people, we should extend the window for casting a ballot to multiple days and locations.

While the traditional practice of voting in person should remain an option, we have the technological capacity to facilitate voting by other means. People should be able to vote by mail, using absentee ballots or other official forms to ensure reliability. In 2000, Oregon became the first state to conduct its presidential election entirely by mail.[1] The secretary of state delivers ballots to all registered voters, who must return their marked ballots by Election Day. Eight states have passed laws to allow elections to be conducted entirely by mail, while others allow mail-only elections in localities.[2] Almost all states allow some form of voting by mail if voters meet certain conditions.

In many other areas of American life, we use online platforms to express preferences and conduct important transactions. You can apply for a passport, purchase a firearm, or enroll in public school using online platforms. We could use similar secure, online processes to facilitate voting — both registering and voting itself. More than twenty states allow their citizens to vote online through secure portals controlled by elections officials.[3] Pursuant to the Uniformed and Overseas Citizens Absentee Voting Act (UOCAVA), members of the US military can cast their ballots online in local and federal elections. If those serving our country in uniform can cast secure ballots, that privilege could be widely extended to all citizens.

It is not only in the method of casting ballots that we should expand access. Many states disqualify categories of people from voting, including those with a felony conviction or certain mental disabilities. People who live legally in this country as permanent non-residents are ineligible to vote, and those who live in US territories like Puerto Rico, Guam, and the US Virgin Islands cannot cast ballots in presidential elections.[4] Regardless of the tremendous impact the executive branch of the federal government has on life in these territories, their residents have no voice in who makes those policies and how they are enacted or implemented.

These rules unduly restrict participation and disenfranchise many people affected by elections. Preventing felons from voting is the most pernicious example of denying individuals a voice and an opportunity for engagement with the political process, since they are among those most directly affected by the laws of this country. Disenfranchisement is one of the many onerous collateral consequences of a felony conviction. The loss of voting rights extends beyond the punishment imposed for the crime and serves no legitimate public safety purpose. It is a categorical exclusion of people who have been otherwise held accountable, unrelated to the facts and circumstances of their criminal conduct. As of 2022, about 4.4 million people lost their right to vote because of a felony conviction.[5] But even that high number is already a 24 percent decrease since 2016, because many legislatures have since recognized the fundamental unfairness of preventing felons from voting and now provide for automatic or discretionary restoration of rights.[6] The exact laws vary from state to state; however, all but nine states have some process for restoration, whether voting is restored after prison, after parole, or after probation.[7] And two states, Vermont and Maine, allow all currently incarcerated prisoners to vote.[8]

As a longtime prosecutor, I am very familiar with the effect of a felony conviction on someone's life even after they have served their sentence. I believe the imposition of onerous collateral consequences on people who have been held accountable and served their time is unfair and counterproductive for both the individuals involved and the larger communities in which they live. Communities are stronger when every member has the ability to be productive and reach their full potential. In pursuit of that goal, I started the Fountain Fund, an organization that provides low-interest loans to formerly incarcerated men and women and helps them reenter communities post-incarceration.[9] We help these individuals access capital to repay court-imposed debt, purchase job-related clothing or equipment, or start small businesses. I believe strongly that we are all invested in the success of returning citizens, as their contributions make our communities stronger. Governments should do more to provide reentry opportunities and help people achieve their full potential.

Participation in government extends beyond voting. There are some traditional models of collective decision making at work in the United States from which we can draw inspiration. For example, Americans have used Quaker meeting rituals and processes as a way of promoting civic engagement and communal decision making since the early days of this country.

The decision-making process is conducted using horizontal leadership. Each person, dubbed a "friend," gets an equal say, and ultimately the group requires a consensus in the final decision. According to the American Friends Service Committee, "In making decisions Friends do not simply vote to determine the majority view, but rather they seek unity about the wisest course of action. Over time Friends have developed ways to conduct meetings that nurture and support this corporate discernment process."[10] Quaker meetings are not just a way of voting but rather a process of how to come to that decision.

This model has already been successfully applied to many modern, secular environments. For example, Quaker schools around the country apply the Quaker method to decision making within their communities, allowing students greater say and transparency in how their own community operates.[11] "The challenges associated with using Quaker processes in a Friends school are often about the time it takes to do justice to the process, as well as our willingness to be transformed by the experience," the Moorestown School writes. "Yet, by leaning into the use of the Quaker process, Friends schools give students the opportunity to try a different way of approaching decision making and give them a set of tools to use throughout their lives."[12]

What would it look like for town councils or other smaller, local-level governments to employ a Quaker model? Could a local school board, for example, implement a process of participatory decision making to decide big issues like the pursuit of particular programs or priorities or more discrete matters like the naming or renaming of a school? If every parent has an opportunity to voice their point of view in this communal process, the end result will reflect a broad consensus and consequently have enhanced legitimacy. Not everyone will necessarily agree with the decision, but they will have had a substantive opportunity to voice their concerns and influence the outcome.

Jury service is another manifestation of citizen participation in government, and, similar to voting, it is infected with exclusions. Most states call people for jury service from voter registration lists, and some pull additional names from the pool of licensed drivers.[13] This process reduces the subset of potential jurors to those who have engaged with other processes of government, leaving large numbers of otherwise eligible citizens outside of the jury process. Almost all states prevent convicted or accused felons from serving on juries.[14] This exclusion suffers from the same fundamental lack of fairness as voting restrictions; these men and women have been held accountable for their crimes and should be able to fully participate in their communities and enjoy all the benefits of citizenship. Facilitating the participation of all citizens in jury service will make the criminal and civil justice systems more democratic.

Some local governments create councils, advisory boards, or other collective processes to collect feedback about specific issues. These panels are often voluntary, allowing individuals to apply to serve. A very timely example of this are police review boards, often called citizens' review boards, which have become even more popular since the summer of 2020 protests. More than 160 towns or cities currently have some form of civilian oversight established through legislation, according to the National Association for Civilian Oversight of Law Enforcement.[15] However, these police oversight boards have vastly different levels of power.[16] According to an ABC News story, "Oversight bodies often face challenges accessing police records, true independence from local politicians, and resistance from police departments and unions, experts say."[17] According to a 2016 report, only 6 percent of civilian oversight agencies have the power to discipline officers, only 40 percent have the ability to subpoena witnesses, and only 41 percent have the ability to subpoena records.[18] Despite these limitations, civilian review boards are an important way to provide accountability, allow for independent investigations, and provide feedback on internal policies and training procedures.

Civilian boards exist across all policy and interest areas. When I first moved to Charlottesville, I applied to serve on the Charlottesville/Albemarle Commission on Children and Families. I had very young children at the time and wanted to contribute to the support our local government provided to our youngest and most vulnerable neighbors. I learned a tremendous amount about my community and was privileged to have a voice in how its resources were deployed. Other popular citizen commissions focus on historic preservation, arts, parks and recreation, ethics, and many other issues. Some larger cities, like New York City, have dozens of such commissions ranging from the Board of Health and City Planning Commission to the Climate Change Adaptation Task Force and the New York Public Library Board.[19] New York City also has general community oversight committees called community boards, whose purpose is "to encourage and facilitate the participation of citizens within city government within their communities, and the efficient and effective organization of agencies that deliver municipal services in local communities and boroughs." There are fifty-nine all-volunteer boards throughout the city, each comprising up to fifty members who are nominated by city council.[20]

Special interest panels are important mechanisms of citizen participation. Governments should look for ways to involve voices from within the communities they serve to help set priorities, guide policymaking, and inform budgetary decisions. These panels are easy to create and require little administrative process and few resources. They give participants a sense of pride in service and broaden the reach of elected officials. Citizen committees are a form of outsourcing that brings important perspectives into conversations about pressing issues, resulting in more representative and effective solutions.

When governments create commissions like the one on which I served, they should cast a wide net for members and ensure the participation of a diverse array of perspectives. These panels often attract people who are already the most informed and able to commit the time and energy to applying and serving. Citizen committees should not rely solely on self-selected volunteers but actively recruit individuals with deep experience and diverse points of view. Service on these panels should accommodate working men and women and others who have limited ability to contribute to such efforts. Citizen commissions need to reflect the communities they serve.

In addition to individuals making efforts to ensure that members of commissions and participants in ad hoc initiatives fully represent communities, the government can also use its resources to back and encourage more civilian participation. In 2011, the Obama administration launched a popular online petitioning platform called "We the People" that allowed anyone to create and support petitions, which would then be reviewed by the administration.[21] This service yielded a number of successful petitions that led to tangible change on topics ranging from state laws banning conversion therapy to baseball legend Yogi Berra receiving the Medal of Freedom.[22]

We should do all we can to promote these mechanisms of citizen involvement and make it easy for all to engage, whether by serving on formal commissions or participating in ad hoc engagement efforts such as circulating petitions or launching letter-writing campaigns. Amnesty International hosts a Write for Rights campaign in the days leading up to World Human Rights Day (December 10) in which people from more than 170 countries are encouraged to write letters and sign petitions for a variety of human-rights-related causes. The campaign netted a stunning 5.8 million letters and signatures in 2023. More important, perhaps, Amnesty International reported that "over 100 people featured in our campaign have seen a positive change in their situation," and the release from imprisonment of at least 48 people could be attributed directly to Write for Rights efforts.[23]

Living in a democracy provides citizens with substantial rights, but also imposes upon them direct responsibilities. It is incumbent upon every American to find ways to participate. The privileges and freedoms we enjoy must be safeguarded through engagement, participation, and attention to the maintenance of those rights. My hope is that the events of Charlottesville and at the Capitol motivate Americans to commit to doing all they can to protect democracy. The simplest and most effective way to achieve that goal is to show up and participate in democratic processes.

20

Constructive Dialogue and Engagement

In addition to encouraging full participation in the various manifestations of democracy, we need to give people the tools to manage the responsibility that comes with such participation. We need to find ways to encourage constructive dialogue among people across this country — within and among communities. We should devise and facilitate systems that help people look beyond the exclusive silos in which they live and get their information and seek out perspectives different from their own. We should help children learn to think critically and navigate the information ecosystem driven by algorithms, affinity groups, and the lack of content moderation among social media platforms. Most important, each of us should find our own unique ways to engage with our neighbors and participate actively in our democracy.

Like many things in life, critical thinking is easier if it's learned and practiced while young. As a threshold step toward creating a more engaged citizenry, we should start with the youngest participants in our democracy — children. Schools have the unique potential to promote the value of community simply by teaching kids how to evaluate information and engage with one another — in other words, teaching them not what to think, but how to think. By giving children the basic skills to navigate life in a pluralistic society, schools plant the seeds that nourish and protect democracy. They should rise to, not shy from, this awesome responsibility and prepare our kids to engage with one another and use the diverse sources of available information. Our schools should help students develop the skills necessary to sift what's true from what's false, to know the difference between verifiable facts and unsubstantiated claims. And they should encourage students to consider alternate perspectives before making decisions or solidifying points of view.

Social media literacy should be a fundamental part of school curriculum. Education about these platforms should start with clarity about how they operate — the practice of curated feeds that respond to prior engagement. We should help kids realize the echo chambers these algorithms create, making it difficult to find and consider alternative perspectives. Schools need to help students understand that traditional sources of news and information are governed by standards different from the free speech platforms of social media. We must prepare our children to navigate a world in which all manner of information is immediately available by pushing a couple of buttons on a device carried in your pocket. These lessons should focus on the benefits these devices and platforms provide as well as their risks. The risk is serious; recently, the US Surgeon General proposed adding a warning label to social media platforms, with a special emphasis alerting parents to the danger they pose to teenagers. Congress would have to approve such an action, but there is precedent, such as warning labels on cigarettes.[1]

Schools should also give our children a framework with which to approach the world. Teachers should expose students to alternative perspectives and ensure that curriculum involves diverse points of view. Schools need to establish mechanisms that encourage students to consider the views of people with whom they disagree and continually hone their opinions. High school students may not remember the specific math formulas or historical facts they are taught, but if they develop the foundational ability to think critically about the world, they will carry that with them forever.

One program tackling both social media and information literacy more broadly is the nonprofit News Literacy Project, whose mission statement reads: "People who are exposed to the News Literacy Project's programs learn how to identify what they can trust, share and act on, and they become better-informed, more engaged and more equal participants in the civic life of their community, their country and the world."[2] Some news organizations, including the *New York Times*, the Associated Press, NPR, Reuters, and many more, have partnered with the program, integrating their content and supporting its mission. The organization targets both educators and students with resources for use in the classroom and beyond. They run a free specialized online learning platform called Checkology, with specific lessons about media sources and bias, misinformation, and even conspiratorial thinking. One version of the platform is designed for younger students, while another has recently launched for adults and the general public, after it became clear how broad the need is.[3] And the program works: 87 percent of students correctly identified fairness as a standard of quality journalism (a 17 percent increase from pre-assessment), 85 percent understood that one of the appeals of conspiracy theories is the sense of community and belonging they provide (a 27 percent increase), and 71 percent of students could recognize when a social media post didn't provide credible evidence (an 8 percent gain).[4]

If there is any environment in which constructive discussion about pressing, complex issues should be possible, it is on college and university campuses. Students should hone their critical thinking skills at the undergraduate college level and emerge with the ability to question assumptions and learn from others. At almost all schools, students with differing social, religious, and cultural backgrounds, and differing political opinions come together in classrooms, dormitories, athletic fields, and dining halls. Many students come to college without prior exposure to ideas and experiences their fellow students have to share, and they generally choose relatively homogeneous work environments, neighborhoods, and social circles when they depart. For most American college students, their time on campus is the best opportunity they will ever have to develop an informed sense of the world's great diversity and their own contributions to it.

The forces of division outlined in this book affect college students as much as the rest of us, and that division prevents some students from embracing the full benefits of living and learning in a diverse college environment. Too many retreat to affinity groups that reinforce rather than challenge their opinions. For some, college is a credential more than an exploration, a way station on a preordained path more than an unpredictable path to self-awareness filled with surprises and marked by personal growth.

To counteract the inertia and division that infects American society and to maximize the collective benefit of the aligned opportunities presented on campus, university leaders need to create systems to encourage critical thinking. This starts with recruiting students and faculty with diverse perspectives — both liberal and conservative. If a particular school, department, or other organization is one-dimensional, it has the tendency to teach more of an orthodoxy than a dynamic understanding of complex issues. Conversely, learning environments in which people with contrasting views can listen to and learn from one another produce more informed students who are prepared to consider all sides of a situation. They will become freethinkers in college and for the rest of their lives, applying the ability to constructively engage when they leave campus and to appreciate the reality that thoughtful people of goodwill can hold conflicting opinions and yet still talk them through, work together, and get along.

At the University of Virginia, where I served as general counsel for three years, several programs aim to encourage respectful dialogue and teach students how to engage with diverse perspectives in a changing world. The university's Miller Center for Public Affairs and Karsh Institute of Democracy have teamed up to establish a series of programs called Democracy Dialogues, which bring together prominent scholars, government officials, and journalists with sharply contrasting views to discuss emerging issues.[5] Professor Mary Kate Cary, a former speechwriter for President George H. W. Bush, directs a program called Think Again UVA, which promotes intellectual diversity on campus. The four pillars of Think Again UVA are freedom of expression, viewpoint diversity, intellectual humility, and critical thinking.[6] Professor Cary regularly works with other faculty with divergent experiences and perspectives to help students come together and practice these core values. Many top universities have launched similar dialogue programs, including Dialogue Vanderbilt, the Project on Civic Dialogue at American University, Harvard Dialogues, and Dean's Dialogue at Yale, the latter of which hosted a candid conversation on Palestine and Israel shortly after the October 7, 2023, attacks.

Even absent a specific campus program, students should pursue opportunities to engage with those with whom they disagree. Diverse perspectives should be abundant on college campuses, and motivated students can and should challenge their own beliefs in exchanges with others of differing views. It is imperative for individual students to take responsibility for their own education by reaching beyond their cocoons of homogeneity. They should embrace their short-lived opportunity to live with and learn from people who come from different backgrounds and hold different views and who are also going through the same process of exploration, learning, and personal growth.

The obligation to seek diverse sources of information and constructively engage with others extends beyond college campuses, though finding and connecting with people with divergent perspectives is perhaps harder outside an academic setting. Interfaith America is one organization facilitating such conversations on a nationwide level through in-person summits and online courses and events, as well as campus and corporate consulting services.[7] Interfaith America says that a five-year longitudinal study of their on-campus program has shown that students involved in it are able to engage productively with others about religious diversity, a first step toward a "thriving, resilient democracy." "While polarization appears to dominate the nation, a majority of Americans want to live in a religiously diverse democracy — though they may lack the skills to unlock that diversity's potential," the organization writes.[8]

While programs like these create important opportunities for constructive dialogue, we cannot sit around and wait for some organized program to come into our lives before we seek to cultivate this crucial life skill. Democracy is stronger if all Americans embrace the opportunity to engage with their diverse peers. All of us need to challenge our assumptions, reach beyond our silos of common information and experience, and think critically. We can do this by seeking out alternative sources of news and information and talking with and listening to friends and neighbors who have different political views. Of course it can be difficult to confront perspectives that sharply differ from your own. But if we approach these encounters with curiosity and humility, we may learn something that enhances our understanding.

21

Pursuing the Common Good

In addition to facilitating dialogue among people who disagree and learning from one another, we need to promote opportunities for Americans to have common experiences. Shared service, collective endeavors, and group pursuit of common interests bring people together like nothing else. Reinforcing our shared humanity by working together is ultimately the most lasting and effective way to strengthen democracy.

I grew up playing team sports from the time I was old enough to run, all the way into college. Sports taught me much about life beyond the fields and courts on which I played. Most important, they taught me how to work with others as part of a team and how to pursue the common goal of winning a game or a championship with a diverse group of others who were committed to the same goal. My high school football team in Fort Washington, Maryland, was, like my high school graduating class, about half white and half Black. We were extremely successful, going undefeated during my senior year until a tough loss in the state championship game. Part of our success stemmed from the personal closeness our team enjoyed off the field. We liked one another, supported one another, and were invested in one another's and the team's success. Some of my teammates lived in areas very different from my suburban street and faced challenges outside of school that I could only imagine. I didn't see some of my teammates in any of my classes, as they struggled in subjects in which I excelled. Outside football, we seemed to have little in common, yet we felt like brothers because we shared a very important, common purpose.

High school football was one of the most formative experiences of my life. It shaped me as much as anything else I did in high school, as it reinforced the power of shared experience. When people come together to pursue a common goal, their differences seem less significant and less divisive. Bringing people together in any group pursuit provides the impetus for them to see one another in ways they would not otherwise. Shared pursuits reveal our essential sameness.

The same thing can happen on a national scale if we create ways for Americans to come together in a common cause, shared service, and collective endeavors. Perhaps Congress could find common ground on a deal to fund national service programs and encourage young people to devote time and energy to fixing the problems in their communities. A huge benefit of a national service program would be that it would bring together young people from disparate backgrounds and regions, as military service already does. Through a national service program, young adults who grew up going to country clubs would work with peers who grew up in public housing, reinforcing their shared values and creating a shared endeavor that decreases distance. National service programs increase civic engagement, benefiting both the beneficiaries of projects and those who are providing the assistance.

There are many recent and current models of national service from which to draw inspiration. In its own words, AmeriCorps is a federal agency that "brings people together to tackle the country's most pressing challenges through national service and volunteering" in communities around the country.[1] The program offers paid and volunteer opportunities to people of all ages to serve on the local, state, and national level in areas of focus ranging from disaster services and education to veterans and military services.[2] And overall, its programs have been successful. The AmeriCorps Office of Research and Evaluation (ORE) recently found a positive effect on measures across student literacy, school attendance, and environmental protection.[3]

The government can incentivize programs like AmeriCorps and other national service programs by providing benefits for those who participate. The Public Service Loan Forgiveness (PSLF) program forgives any outstanding balance from the Department of Education if you work ten years full-time at certain nonprofit or government agencies and make qualified payments toward your loans. In March 2025, President Trump issued an executive order eliminating eligibility for some organizations, but AmeriCorps service still counts toward this ten-year period.[4] Federal or state governments could similarly provide direct stipends, tax credits, tuition vouchers, or other forms of financial or other support for those who enroll in national service programs.

Retired general Stanley McChrystal served as commander of the International Security Assistance Force in Afghanistan. He has proposed a national service requirement as a condition of citizenship as a "big idea" designed to foster American unity and democracy.[5] McChrystal's proposal would require Americans to provide one year of service, doing things like tutoring students in under-performing schools, caring for elderly residents in nursing homes, or providing disaster relief in distressed communities. Military service would also count toward this requirement, though only as one of many options available for individuals to choose from. It is not surprising that a thirty-four-year veteran of the armed forces like General McChrystal would support this kind of effort, as the military, like my high school sports experience, is another example of unity achieved through common purpose. While imposing a mandatory service obligation may be difficult to achieve politically, some studies have shown that it would be popular.[6]

Many countries require some form of military service. According to studies by the Centre for Economic Policy Research, "military conscription contributed to the formation of a shared national identity, boosting loyalty to the polity, and instilling patriotism."[7]

But a deliberate commitment to pursuing the common good should not be solely reserved for young people enrolled in government-sanctioned programs. All Americans can implement this priority in their lives by seeking opportunities to work toward community or other shared goals and objectives. Schools, churches, neighborhoods, any number of various organizations all set goals for the benefit of their members. Participating in these collective efforts and working with others in pursuit of those goals has tremendous benefits beyond making progress toward achieving the goal that is being pursued. Coming together with our neighbors to build a playground, working with other parents to fund an after-school program, or joining a church group on a service trip to a faraway place all enhance our understanding of our place in the world and the people with whom we interact. These efforts connect us to something larger and represent an affirmative antidote to division in America.

22

Let Us All Recommit

The prospective reforms I've suggested won't cure the division that afflicts our democracy. They will, however, mitigate its effects and limit its reach. Given the paralysis of government, we must all take on democracy as a common project and approach the maintenance of our democracy as a shared responsibility. The more people participate in the processes of government and the workings of their communities, listen to and engage with people with differing views, and pursue shared experience and common purpose, the stronger our democracy will be.

The complex challenges we face in this country and the forces that infect our current system are daunting and intimidating. It's tempting to ask oneself "How can I fix this?" and struggle to find good answers. My strong advice is to go micro, not macro. Our approach to fixing those problems and protecting democracy should start with each of us, in our own small ways, committing to do the daily work that democracy demands. Educate yourself. Find ways to connect with others and find common purpose. Vote. Daily, individual choices have ripple effects and create a more just, humane, and democratic society. If each of us commits to doing our own part, we can and will circumvent the division that afflicts America today and heal our fractured country.

Despite the hard-earned lessons of my work on the events in Charlottesville and on January 6, I remain optimistic about our ability to protect democracy. The approaches outlined above really are quite simple, and therefore achievable, if we muster the will to overcome our own apathy. I believe that people are fundamentally good, motivated largely by benign impulses, and influenced profoundly by the joy and pain of the people around them. While there are systemic impediments pulling us apart and profiting from the divide, there are more powerful forces — our humanity and our legacy of democracy — that will keep us together if we make the effort.

The spasms of political violence in Charlottesville and on January 6 were harbingers of American polarization and our dangerous potential to descend into conflict and division. Those events were America at its worst. Let us respond by reaffirming America at its best. We should see Charlottesville and January 6 as motivators and use them to make us stronger. Let them encourage us all to recommit to preserving American democracy.